Mathematics

Revision Notes
For GCSE

P. JENKINS

Schofield & Sims Ltd · Huddersfield

0 7217 2298 9
First printed 1980
Reprinted 1981
Revised and reprinted 1986

ACKNOWLEDGEMENT

The author wishes to acknowledge her indebtedness to
Mrs. K. Malcolm, and to other members of the
Mathematics Department of St. Joseph's High School
for their help: Mr. N. Stephenson, Dr. A. R. Cooke and
Mr. M. C. Jones.

Printed in England by Martin's of Berwick

USING THIS BOOK

It is assumed that you already have experience of the Mathematics to which these notes can be applied. All the fundamentals are here, but stated briefly to enable you to memorise them and so readily call to mind the information required for a particular problem.

PART ONE contains all the *basic* rules necessary for GCSE.

PART TWO contains additional material that you will need if you are hoping to achieve the highest grades.

CONTENTS

CONTENTS

Part Two—Additional material essential for the highest grades

SYMBOLS

Make sure you are familiar with the following:

$>$	is greater than
$=$	is equal to
$<$	is less than
$\geqslant$	is greater than or equal to
$\leqslant$	is less than or equal to
$\neq$	is not equal to
$\approx$ or $\simeq$	is approximately equal to
$\equiv$	is equivalent to
$\therefore$	therefore
$\because$	because
$/\!/$	is parallel to
$\perp$	is perpendicular to
$\overrightarrow{AB}$ $\mathbf{AB}$	} the vector $\mathbf{AB}$
N	the set of natural numbers
$\mathscr{E}$	the universal set
$\cap$	the intersection of
$\cup$	the union of
$A \subset B$	'A' is contained in 'B' *or* 'A' is a subset of 'B'
$A \supset B$	'A' contains 'B' *or* 'B' is a subset of 'A'
$\subseteq$ $\supseteq$	} is a subset of or equals
$\{\ \}$ or $\varnothing$	the empty set
$\in$	belongs to (is a member of)
$\notin$	is not a member of
$n(A)$	number of elements in a set (A)
A'	complement of A
$a \Rightarrow b$	'a' implies 'b'
$a \Leftarrow b$	'b' implies 'a'
$a \Leftrightarrow b$	'a' implies 'b' and 'b' implies 'a'

Part One

ARITHMETIC

Four rules of number for whole numbers

Addition (+)	Subtraction (−)	Multiplication (×)

Division (÷)

Factors
A factor is a number which will divide exactly into another number.

Prime Numbers
A prime number is divisible only by itself and 1.

These numbers are 2, 3, 5, 7, 11, 13 etc.

Therefore a **prime factor** is a factor which is also a prime number.

Example 1.

Prime factors of 270.

```
  * 
2 |270
3 |135
3 | 45
3 | 15
5 |  5
  |  1
```

Remember to divide by each prime factor repeatedly until the number will no longer divide exactly, before moving on to the next one. The numbers in the * column now give the prime factors of 270.

Prime factors are $2 \times 3 \times 3 \times 3 \times 5$

or in index form $2 \times 3^3 \times 5$.

Example 2.

Prime factors of 325.

```
   * 
 5 |325
 5 | 65
13 | 13
   |  1
```

Prime factors are $5 \times 5 \times 13$

or in index form $5^2 \times 13$.

7

Highest Common Factor (H.C.F.)

This is the highest factor common to a group of numbers. First reduce the numbers to their prime factors; then the H.C.F. can easily be seen.

e.g. H.C.F. of 28, 140 and 56.

The numbers in the * columns are the prime factors of each number.

$$\begin{array}{r|r} & * \\ 2 & 28 \\ \hline 2 & 14 \\ \hline 7 & 7 \\ \hline & 1 \end{array} \qquad \begin{array}{r|r} & * \\ 2 & 140 \\ \hline 2 & 70 \\ \hline 5 & 35 \\ \hline 7 & 7 \\ \hline & 1 \end{array} \qquad \begin{array}{r|r} & * \\ 2 & 56 \\ \hline 2 & 28 \\ \hline 2 & 14 \\ \hline 7 & 7 \\ \hline & 1 \end{array}$$

$28 = 2^2 \times 7$

$140 = 2^2 \times 5 \times 7$

$56 = 2^3 \times 7$

H.C.F. is $2^2 \times 7 = 4 \times 7 = 28.$

Lowest Common Multiple (L.C.M.)

This is the lowest number divisible by each member of the group. The division by the prime factors can be done collectively.

e.g. L.C.M. of 14, 18 and 21.

$$\begin{array}{r|rrr} & * \\ 2 & 14, & 18, & 21 \\ \hline 3 & 7, & 9, & 21 \\ \hline 3 & 7, & 3, & 7 \\ \hline 7 & 7, & 1, & 7 \\ \hline & 1, & 1, & 1 \end{array}$$

Where a number is not divisible by the prime number it is repeated on the line below.

The product of the numbers in the * column gives the L.C.M. of the group of numbers.

L.C.M. is $2 \times 3^2 \times 7 = 126.$

Vulgar Fractions

e.g. $\dfrac{3}{8}$ ← Numerator
      ← Denominator

The denominator indicates the number of parts the 'whole' quantity is divided into. The numerator indicates the number of these parts.

Terms used: Proper fractions, e.g. $\frac{2}{3}$; Improper fractions, e.g. $\frac{14}{3}$;

Mixed numbers, e.g. $2\frac{5}{8}$.

Mixed numbers can be converted into improper fractions,

e.g. $2\frac{5}{8} = \frac{21}{8}$.

Likewise, improper fractions can be converted into mixed numbers,

e.g. $\frac{14}{3} = 4\frac{2}{3}$.

Addition and Subtraction

For addition and subtraction the fractions can be left as mixed numbers. The whole numbers can be added or subtracted first and the fractional parts can then be dealt with by converting them into fractions with the same denominator, i.e. by finding the L.C.M. of the denominators.

Example 1.

$$3\frac{4}{7} + 2\frac{3}{14}$$
$$= 5\frac{8+3}{14}$$
$$= 5\frac{11}{14}$$

Example 2.

$$3\frac{5}{8} - 1\frac{1}{6}$$
$$= 2\frac{15-4}{24}$$
$$= 2\frac{11}{24}$$

In an example such as $\quad 8\frac{1}{6} - 3\frac{8}{9}$

change one unit into $\frac{1}{18}$ths in order to do the subtraction.

$$= 5\frac{3-16}{18}$$
$$= 4\frac{21-16}{18}$$
$$= 4\frac{5}{18}$$

Multiplication and Division

Always work in the form of improper fractions.

Example 1.

$$5\frac{1}{8} \times 1\frac{3}{5}$$
$$= \frac{41}{8_1} \times \frac{8^1}{5}$$
$$= \frac{41}{5}$$
$$= 8\frac{1}{5}$$

Example 2.

$$6\frac{2}{3} \div 2\frac{1}{7}$$
$$= \frac{20}{3} \div \frac{15}{7}$$

Change sign and turn fraction upside-down.

$$= \frac{20^4}{3} \times \frac{7}{15_3}$$
$$= \frac{28}{9}$$
$$= 3\frac{1}{9}$$

9

Rules for Fractions involving Several Operations

1. Brackets take precedence, i.e. whatever is in brackets should be worked out first.
2. If there are no brackets, then multiplication and division signs take precedence over addition and subtraction signs.

Example 1.

$$\tfrac{1}{3} + (\tfrac{3}{5} - \tfrac{1}{2}) \times \tfrac{5}{6} \qquad \longleftarrow \text{ Brackets take precedence.}$$

$$= \tfrac{1}{3} + \left(\tfrac{6-5}{10}\right) \times \tfrac{5}{6}$$

$$= \tfrac{1}{3} + \tfrac{1}{\cancel{10}_2} \times \tfrac{\cancel{5}^1}{6} \qquad \longleftarrow \text{ Multiplication sign takes precedence.}$$

$$= \tfrac{1}{3} + \tfrac{1}{12}$$

$$= \tfrac{4+1}{12} = \tfrac{5}{12}$$

Example 2. In a complex fraction do *not* separate the numerator and denominator; evaluate both at the same time.

$$\frac{3\tfrac{1}{2} \div \tfrac{7}{10} - 2\tfrac{1}{8} \times \tfrac{4}{5}}{\tfrac{1}{4} + 2\tfrac{1}{2} + 1\tfrac{3}{5}} \qquad \longleftarrow \begin{array}{l}\text{Multiplication and division signs take}\\\text{precedence.}\end{array}$$

$$= \frac{\dfrac{\cancel{7}^1}{2_1} \times \dfrac{\cancel{10}^5}{\cancel{7}_1} - \dfrac{17}{\cancel{8}_2} \times \dfrac{\cancel{4}^1}{5}}{3\dfrac{5+10+12}{20}}$$

$$= \frac{5 - 1\tfrac{7}{10}}{4\tfrac{7}{20}}$$

$$= \frac{3\tfrac{3}{10}}{4\tfrac{7}{20}}$$

$$= \frac{\cancel{33}^{11}}{\cancel{10}_1} \times \frac{\cancel{20}^2}{\cancel{87}_{29}} = \frac{22}{29}$$

To Find a Fraction of a Quantity

Multiply the quantity by the fraction.

e.g. $\tfrac{5}{6}$ of an hour $= \tfrac{5}{\cancel{6}_1} \times \cancel{60}^{10}$ minutes $= 50$ minutes

and

$\tfrac{7}{8}$ of £6 $= \tfrac{7}{\cancel{8}_2} \times \cancel{600}^{150}$ pence $= \tfrac{1050}{2} = 525$ pence $= £5 \cdot 25$.

Decimal Fractions

Decimals are fractions which have denominators of 10, 100, 1000, etc., i.e. they are fractions whose denominators are always powers of 10.

e.g. $\quad 0.3 = \frac{3}{10}$; $\quad 0.86 = \frac{86}{100}$; $\quad 9.289 = 9\frac{289}{1000}$.

N.B. When there are no whole numbers, a zero should be inserted in front of the decimal point.

Multiplication and Division by Powers of Ten
The figures will remain unchanged except for the addition of noughts where necessary but the position of the decimal point will alter.

Multiplication
$5.14 \times 10 = 51.4$ decimal point moves *one* place to the right.
$5.14 \times 100 = 514.0$ decimal point moves *two* places to the right.
$5.14 \times 1000 = 5140.0$ decimal point moves *three* places to the right, and so on.

Division
$468.3 \div 10 = 46.83$ decimal point moves *one* place to the left.
$468.3 \div 100 = 4.683$ decimal point moves *two* places to the left.
$468.3 \div 1000 = 0.4683$ decimal point moves *three* places to the left, and so on.

To Convert Vulgar Fractions to Decimal Fractions
Divide the numerator by the denominator.

e.g.   Express $\frac{7}{8}$ as a decimal.

```
      0.875
   8 │ 7.000
      6 4
      ────
        60
        56
        ──
        40
        40
        ··
```

$$\therefore \frac{7}{8} = 0.875$$

Addition and Subtraction of Decimals
Care must be taken to ensure that the decimal points are underneath one another so that the figures in each column have the same place value.

e.g. $25.6 + 19 + 364.23 =$ 25.6
                                 19.0
                               364.23
                               _____
                               408.83

Multiplication and Division of Decimals

Multiply as if the numbers are whole numbers but, when the final answer has been reached, count the number of figures after the decimal points in the question, and make sure you place the point in the answer so that there are the same number of figures *after* the point in the answer.

e.g.   136.4
             2.3 ⟵ 2 figures after the point in the question
           _____
           27280   ↓
            4092   tenths × tenths give hundredths
           _____
           313.72   Place the point here so that there are 2 figures
                     after the point in the answer.

When dividing, make the divisor (the number being divided by) a whole number by multiplying by the appropriate power of 10, and make sure the same alteration is made to the number being divided into. This means the relationship between the numbers has not been altered.

e.g. $9.662 \div 3.5$ 2.76
                             35$\overline{)96.62}$
         $= 96.62 \div 35$ 70
                              _____
                               26 6
                               24 5   Answer:
                              _____   2.8 to one place of
                               2 12   decimals.
                               2 10
                              _____
                                 2

To Express one Quantity as a Decimal of another

1. If necessary, change both quantities into the same unit.
2. Write as a vulgar fraction and then convert to a decimal fraction in the usual way.

e.g.   Express 75p as a decimal fraction of £15.

$$\tfrac{75}{1500} = 75 \div 1500 = 0.75 \div 15 = 0.05$$

Number Bases

The number system used every day is base 10, or the denary system, i.e. counting in groups of 10. However, there is nothing to prevent counting being done in groups of 2, 3, 4, 5, 6, etc.

16 base 10 means 1 group of 10 and 6 extra. To change it into a number base 3, group the 16 in threes. This means 1 group of '3 threes', 2 groups of three and 1 extra.

i.e. $16_{10} = 121_3$ N.B. the base being used is recorded as a small number at the foot of the figures.

To change a decimal number (denary number) to any other base, simply divide by the base and record the remainders.

e.g.   Express 59_{10} in base three.

$$
\begin{array}{r|l}
3 & 59 \\
3 & 19 \quad \text{remainder 2} \\
3 & 6 \quad \text{remainder 1} \\
3 & 2 \quad \text{remainder 0} \uparrow \\
& 0 \quad \text{remainder 2}
\end{array}
$$

The remainders, read from the bottom up, now give the required answer.

i.e. $59_{10} = 2012_3$

To change a number in another base back to base 10, only the place values of the digits making up the number need to be remembered. When counting in tens, the pattern is as follows:

← and so on	Thousands	Hundreds	Tens	Units
	10^3	10^2	10	1

∴   The pattern for other bases will be similar.

e.g.   The pattern for base three will be:

← and so on	3^3	3^2	3	Units

Change 2012_3 into base 10.

3^3	3^2	3	Units
2	0	1	2

The number to base 10 will then be: $2(3)^3 + 0(3)^2 + 1(3) + 2(1)$

$$= 54 + 0 + 3 + 2 = 59_{10}.$$

The base most commonly used besides 10 is base 2 (binary numbers). Binary numbers will be made up entirely of 'ones' and 'zeros'.

Change 47_{10} to base 2.

$$47_{10} = 101111_2$$

2	47	
2	23	remainder 1
2	11	remainder 1
2	5	remainder 1
2	2	remainder 1 ↑
2	1	remainder 0
	0	remainder 1

Change 101111_2 to denary.

2^5	2^4	2^3	2^2	2	Units
1	0	1	1	1	1

$$= 32 + 0 + 8 + 4 + 2 + 1 = 47_{10}$$

Addition and Subtraction in Bases other than Ten

The ordinary processes of addition and subtraction are carried out in the same manner as in base ten, but extra care must be taken when 'carrying' to remember the base in which the work is being done.

Example 1.

Add 123_8 and 237_8.

$$\begin{array}{r} 123 \\ + 237 \\ \hline 362_8 \end{array}$$

$7 + 3 = 10$
$= 1$ group of 8 to 'carry' and 2 left to put in the first column of the answer.

Example 2.

From 23_5 subtract 14_5.

$$\begin{array}{r} 23 \\ - 14 \\ \hline 4_5 \end{array}$$

Remember when 'borrowing' that a bundle of 5 is being borrowed.

Multiplication and Division in Bases other than Ten

When working in bases other than ten, multiply and divide in the usual way, but remember to apply the new tables.

e.g. $213_5 \times 24_5$

$$\begin{array}{r} 213 \\ 24 \\ \hline 4310 \\ 1412 \\ \hline 11222_5 \end{array}$$

$4 \times 3 = 12 = 22_5$

14

Examples of the four rules applied to binary numbers.

1. $1011_2 + 111_2 + 10110_2 + 1111_2$ 2. $10110_2 - 1011_2$

$$
\begin{array}{r}
1011 \\
111 \\
10110 \\
+\ 1111 \\
\hline
110111_2
\end{array}
\qquad
\begin{array}{r}
10110 \\
-\ 1011 \\
\hline
1011_2
\end{array}
$$

3. $1011_2 \times 101_2$ 4. $1000001_2 \div 101_2$

$$
\begin{array}{r}
1011 \\
101 \\
\hline
101100 \\
1011 \\
\hline
110111_2
\end{array}
$$

$$
\begin{array}{r}
1101_2 \\
101\,\overline{)\,1000001} \\
101 \\
\hline
110 \\
101 \\
\hline
101 \\
101 \\
\hline
\end{array}
$$

Approximations

By taking suitable approximations to the numbers in a calculation a rough check can be made. Such a check is likely to show up any mistakes in the position of the decimal point.

Thus for the calculation $4261 \times 76 = 323\,836,$

a rough check could be $4000 \times 80 = 320\,000.$

Also, for $\dfrac{418\,095}{815} = 513,$

a rough check could be $\dfrac{400\,000}{800} = 500.$

Significant Figures (abbrev. SF)

The first non-zero digit on the left of a number is called the first significant figure. A number will be 'correct to 1 significant figure' if there is only one 'significant figure'.

e.g. $2367 = 2000$, correct to 1 significant figure.

        $0.325 = 0.3$, correct to 1 significant figure.

If the second digit is greater than or equal to 5, then the number is corrected 'up', e.g. $467 = 500$, correct to 1 significant figure.

If more than 1 significant figure is required, then all figures, including zeros, after the first non-zero digit must be counted.

Example 1. $56\,093 = 60\,000$ correct to 1 SF

$= 56\,000$ correct to 2 SF

$= 56\,100$ correct to 3 SF

$= 56\,090$ correct to 4 SF.

Example 2. $0.002486 = 0.002$ correct to 1 SF

$= 0.0025$ correct to 2 SF

$= 0.00249$ correct to 3 SF.

Decimal Places

To determine the number of decimal places, start counting at the decimal point.

e.g. $0.02473 = 0.02$ correct to 2 decimal places

$= 0.025$ correct to 3 decimal places

$= 0.0247$ correct to 4 decimal places.

Notice that zeros after the decimal point are counted.

Averages

To find the average of a number of quantities, add the quantities together and divide the total by the number of quantities.

e.g. Find the average age of three boys aged 5 years 6 months, 6 years 2 months, and 5 years 11 months.

Total age $= 17$ years 7 months.

$$\text{Average age} = \frac{17 \text{ yrs. } 7 \text{ mths.}}{3}$$

$$\approx 5 \text{ years } 10 \text{ months.}$$

$$\text{Average} = \frac{\text{Total}}{\text{No. of quantities}}$$

> Average × no. of quantities = Total.
>
> Do not confuse with average speed which means the distance travelled in *one* hour.
>
> i.e.   Average Speed $= \dfrac{\text{Distance}}{\text{Time (in hours)}}$

Ratio

A ratio is a comparison between two similar quantities.

e.g. If there are 30 apples and 5 oranges, then the ratio of apples to oranges is $\dfrac{30}{5} = \dfrac{6}{1}$ or 6:1.

In other words, there are 6 apples for every one orange.

As indicated, a ratio may be expressed as a fraction, i.e. $2:8 = \dfrac{2}{8}$; and a ratio can be cancelled down like a fraction, i.e. $\dfrac{2}{8} = \dfrac{1}{4}$.

Before a ratio can be stated, the units of the quantities must be the same.

e.g. the ratio between 36p and £9 is 36p:900p which equals 1:25 in its simplest form.

To divide an amount in a given ratio

e.g. £30 is divided in the ratio 3:5:7; calculate each share.

Add the ratio parts together. $(3 + 5 + 7 = 15$ parts$)$

$$15 \text{ parts} \equiv £30 \quad 1 \text{ part} \equiv £2$$

∴ 3 parts ≡ £6 ; 5 parts ≡ £10 ; 7 parts ≡ £14

Proportion

1. *Direct Proportion*   Two quantities are said to vary directly, or be in direct proportion, if they increase or decrease at the same rate. If 10 metres of material are needed to make 2 dresses, then 20 metres will be needed to make 4 dresses, and 5 metres will be needed to make 1 dress. That is, if the number of dresses made is doubled, then double the amount of material will be needed; if the number of dresses made is halved, the amount of material needed will be halved.

There are two methods that can be used when solving problems on direct proportion: the unitary method or the fractional method.

e.g.   If 36 articles cost £72, what will 40 articles cost?

(a) *Unitary method*   36 articles cost £72

$$1 \text{ article costs } \frac{£72}{36} = £2$$

$$\therefore \text{ 40 articles cost } £2 \times 40 = £80.$$

(b) *Fractional method*   Cost of 40 articles $= \dfrac{40}{\cancel{36}} \times £\cancel{72}^{2} = £80.$

2. *Inverse Proportion*   Suppose 12 men working on a certain job take 20 days to complete it. If the number of men working on the job is doubled then the job should take half the time. If the number of men is halved then the job will probably take twice as long. This is an example of inverse proportion.
    e.g. If 30 men produce 1000 articles in 8 days, how long will 40 men take to produce the same amount?

Here the number of men is *increased* in the ratio $\dfrac{40}{30} = \dfrac{4}{3}$, so this is an example of inverse proportion and the number of days required will be *decreased* in the ratio $\dfrac{3}{4}$.

$$\therefore \text{ Number of days required} = \frac{3}{\cancel{4}_{1}} \times \cancel{8}^{2}$$

$$= 6 \text{ days.}$$

Percentages
The words 'per cent' mean 'per 100'.

To convert a percentage to a fraction divide by 100

e.g.   40% as a vulgar fraction $= \frac{40}{100} = \frac{4}{10} \left(\frac{2}{5}\right)$.

40% as a decimal fraction $= 40 \div 100 = 0.40$.

To convert a fraction to a percentage multiply by 100

e.g. $\frac{3}{20}$ as a percentage $= \frac{3}{20} \times 100 = 15\%$.

0.418 as a percentage $= 0.418 \times 100 = 41.8\%$.

To express one quantity as a percentage of another express as a fraction and convert

e.g. £9 as a percentage of £300

$$= \frac{9}{300} \times 100 = 3\%.$$

i.e. first express the £9 as a fraction of the £300; then convert the fraction to a percentage.

N.B. In examples of this type the units of the quantities must be the same.

e.g. 35 centimetres as a percentage of 4 metres

$$= \frac{35}{400} \times 100 = \frac{35}{4} = 8\frac{3}{4}\%.$$

Percentages of Quantities

e.g. 15% of £9 $= \dfrac{15}{100} \times 900$ pence $= 135$ pence $= £1\cdot35.$

Profit and Loss

C.P. = cost price ; S.P. = selling price.

Actual profit or loss = the difference between S.P. and C.P.

$$\% \text{ profit} = \frac{\text{Actual profit}}{\text{C.P.}} \times 100 \quad ; \quad \% \text{ loss} = \frac{\text{Actual loss}}{\text{C.P.}} \times 100.$$

Example 1.

An article bought for £20 is sold for £21·80; find the percentage profit.

C.P. = £20 $\% \text{ profit} = \dfrac{180}{2000} \times 100$

S.P. = £21·80 $= 9\%$ profit.

Actual profit = £1·80

Example 2.

A book is bought for 50p and sold for 40p; find the percentage loss.

C.P. = 50p $\% \text{ loss} = \dfrac{10}{50} \times 100$

S.P. = 40p $= \dfrac{1}{5} \times 100$

Actual loss = 10p $= 20\%$ loss

Interest

When money is invested, interest is paid to the investor. Likewise, when money is borrowed, the person who borrows the money will have to pay interest to the lender. The amount of money which is invested or lent is called the *Principal* and the charge made for lending it is called the *Interest*. The percentage return is called the 'rate per cent'. A rate of 8% means that for every £100 invested or lent the interest will be £8 per year. The principal plus the interest is known as the *Amount*.

Simple Interest

With simple interest the principal always stays the same no matter how many years the investment or the loan lasts.

Simple interest can be calculated using direct proportion. However, this method gives rise to a very simple formula that can be memorised:

$$S.I. = \frac{P \times R \times T}{100}$$
where P = principal; R = rate of interest (%); T = time in years; and S.I. = simple interest.

Amount = Principal + Interest

Manipulation of formula to find P or R or T gives:

$$P = \frac{100 \times S.I.}{T \times R} \quad ; \quad R = \frac{100 \times S.I.}{P \times T} \quad ; \quad T = \frac{100 \times S.I.}{P \times R}$$

Compound Interest

With compound interest the principal is increased by the addition of the interest whenever this is due (yearly or otherwise), and since the principal increases, the annual interest will also increase.

When the period of time is short the calculation of compound interest is done as repeated simple interest.

e.g.　Find the compound interest on £550 for 2 years at 5% per annum (p.a.).

Principal for 1st. year	£550·00
Interest for 1st. year	27·50
Principal for 2nd. year	£577·50
Interest for 2nd. year	28·875
Amount	£606·375

Compound Interest = Amount − Principal
$$= £606{\cdot}375 - £550 = £56{\cdot}375 \approx £56{\cdot}38$$

There is a formula that can be used if period of time is excessive:

The amount after 'n' years is $P\left(1 + \dfrac{r}{100}\right)^n$ where P is the principal and 'r' is rate per cent per annum,

i.e. $A = P\left(1 + \dfrac{r}{100}\right)^n.$

e.g. Calculate the compound interest on £384·50 for 5 years at 3% per annum.

$$A = P\left(1 + \frac{r}{100}\right)^n$$

$$A = 384{\cdot}50\left(1 + \frac{3}{100}\right)^5$$

$$A = 384{\cdot}50 \, (1.03)^5$$

∴ Amount by calculator ≈ £445·74

∴ Compound Interest ≈ £445·74 − £384·50 ≈ £61·24.

Perimeter
This is the total distance around the outer edge of a shape.

Example 1.

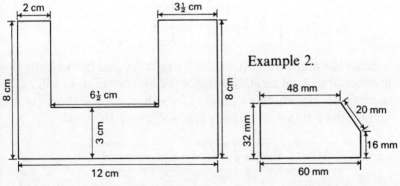

Example 2.

In Example 1, perimeter $= 8 + 12 + 8 + 2 + 5 + 6\frac{1}{2} + 5 + 3\frac{1}{2}$ cm
$= 50$ cm.

In Example 2, perimeter $= 60 + 32 + 48 + 20 + 16$ mm
$= 176$ mm.

21

Circumference

The perimeter of a circle is known as the *circumference* and it is easy to show by experiment that there is a special relationship between the circumference and the diameter of a circle. The circumference is approximately *three* times the diameter regardless of the size of the circle. Since this is a constant it has been given the special symbol π (the Greek letter pi). Although π has no exact value, for most calculations it is sufficiently accurate to use the values 3.14 or $\frac{22}{7}$.

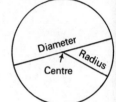

$$\frac{\text{Circumference of circle}}{\text{Diameter (d)}} = \pi$$

$\therefore$ Circumference of circle = πd or 2πr
(since diameter = 2 × radius)

Area

Area means amount of surface and is measured in square units.

Area of Rectangle

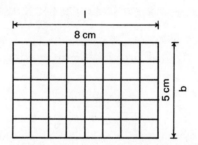

Since the number of squares in a row will equal numerically the number of units of length and since the number of rows will equal numerically the number of units of width, there is a short cut for finding the number of squares that will cover the surface.

i.e. | Area of Rectangle = l × b square units |

Area of Parallelogram   Any parallelogram can be shown to be equal in area to a rectangle with the same base and the same perpendicular height; hence its area equals base × perpendicular height.

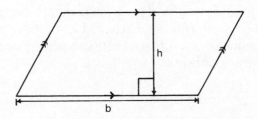

i.e. | Area of Parallelogram = b × h square units |

Area of Triangle Any triangle can be shown to be equal to half the area of a rectangle with the same base and the same perpendicular height; hence its area equals half base × perpendicular height.

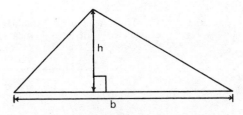

i.e. | Area of Triangle = $\frac{1}{2}$b × h square units |

Area of Trapezium Any trapezium can be divided into two triangles with equal heights:

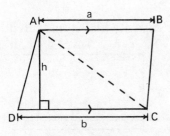

i.e. | Area of Trapezium = $\frac{1}{2}$(sum of parallel sides) × the perpendicular distance between them.
i.e. $\frac{1}{2}$(a + b) × h square units. |

23

Area of Circle It is easy to show by experiment that not only is the ratio between the area of a circle and its (radius)^2 a constant, but it is the same constant that exists between the circumference and the diameter, namely π.

$$\frac{\text{Area of Circle}}{(\text{radius})^2} = \pi$$

i.e.   Area of Circle $= \pi r^2$ square units

Surface Area of a Cylinder

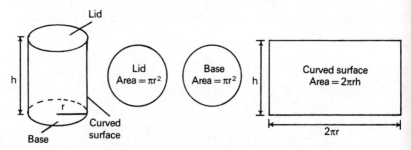

Total surface area of closed cylinder $= 2\pi r^2 + 2\pi rh$

$\qquad\qquad\qquad\qquad\qquad\quad = 2\pi r(r+h)$ square units.

Total surface area of open cylinder $= \pi r^2 + 2\pi rh$

$\qquad\qquad\qquad\qquad\qquad\quad = \pi r(r+2h)$ square units.

Volume
Volume is space or capacity and is measured in cubic units.

Volume of Box

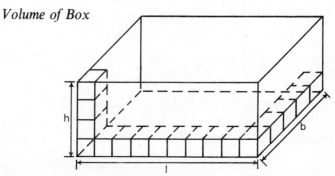

The number of cubes that will cover the floor of the box can be found by multiplying the number of units of length by the number of units of width, the reason being the same as that which led to the short cut for finding the area of a rectangle. The number of layers of cubes necessary to fill the box will be the same numerically as the number of units of height and this gives a short cut for finding the number of cubes that will fill the box.

i.e.

> Volume of box $= l \times b \times h$ cubic units

Since the first part of the formula, namely $l \times b$, gives the area of the base or cross-section, this leads to a more general formula for the volume of any figure that has uniform cross-section.

> Volume of anything with uniform cross-section =
> area of cross-section × height (or length)

Volume of Prism

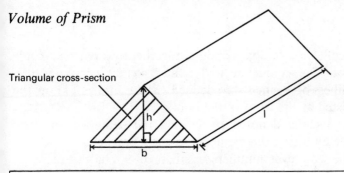

Triangular cross-section

> Volume of prism $= (\frac{1}{2}b \times h) \times l$ cubic units

Volume of Swimming-pool (Solid with Trapezoid cross-section)

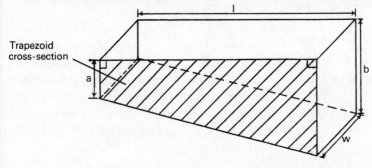

Trapezoid cross-section

25

> Volume of solid $= \frac{1}{2}(a + b) \times l \times w$ cubic units

Volume of Cylinder

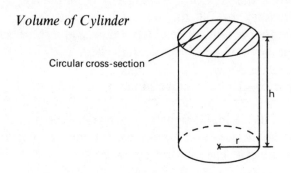

Circular cross-section

> Volume of cylinder $= \pi r^2 h$ cubic units

Sets

A set is a collection of objects bound together by a particular rule or definition. The set must be 'well-defined' so that it contains only those members or 'elements' so defined. (Make sure you know the symbols listed at the front of the book.)

A set is usually denoted by writing the definition in curly brackets or by listing the members in curly brackets.

e.g. 'A is the set of even numbers less than 10' can be written:

$$A = \{\text{even numbers less than } 10\},$$

or $\quad A = \{2,4,6,8\}.$

Then $2 \in A$ means 2 'is a member of' A.

Finite and Infinite Sets

Set A above is a *finite* set, i.e. there is a limit to the number of elements of the set. If set B is the set of even numbers greater than 1 and less than 60, then this is also a finite set but there are too many members or elements to list easily. This can be written: $B = \{2,4,6, \cdots, 58\}$, using a row of dots to indicate the members which are understood but not listed.

However, if the definition of a set C is 'the set of all even numbers' then the list of elements is endless, i.e. this set has no limit and is said to be *infinite*. This can be written: $C = \{2,4,6,\cdots\}$, again using dots to indicate the unlisted members.

The important thing is that a finite set must show the last member whereas an infinite set cannot.

Empty Sets

Consider the set of 'live' volcanoes in Britain. Since there are no members of this set it is said to be an empty or null set and is written as $\emptyset$ or { }. Do not confuse the empty set, which means there are *no* elements in the set, with {0} which means there *is* an element which is the zero quantity.

Subsets

If set A is the set of whole numbers less than or equal to 10 ($\leqslant 10$) and then set B is taken as the set of even numbers $\leqslant 10$, then B is part of the larger set A, i.e. B is a subset of A, or $B \subset A$.

A *proper subset* is one which does not contain all the elements of the original set. For example, consider the set {apple, orange}. The subsets are (i) { }, (ii) {apple}, (iii) {orange}, (iv) {apple, orange}; but only (i), (ii) and (iii) are proper subsets.

Equal and Equivalent Sets

Two sets are said to be equal if every element of the first set is a member of the second set and every element of the second set is a member of the first set.

e.g.   {cat, dog, mouse} = {dog, mouse, cat}

(Remember, the order of the elements is unimportant.)

Sets are said to be equivalent if they have different elements but the same number of elements (i.e. the elements can be paired).

e.g. {knife, fork, spoon} and {cup, saucer, plate} are equivalent. Both contain 3 elements.

The Universal Set ($\mathscr{E}$)

Consider the 'set of all trees' or 'the set of all dogs'; large sets of this kind are called 'universal sets'.

However, a universal set does not necessarily include all possible elements. In a mathematical problem the universal set can be restricted to the set of all elements required in the particular problem.

Union (∪)

The union of two sets is the combination of two sets, and often the sets will have elements in common.

e.g. $A = \{1,3,5,7\}$, $B = \{5,7,10,14\}$

∴ $A \cup B = \{1,3,5,7,10,14\}$

In diagram form this can be represented as:

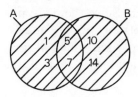

i.e. The union set consists of all the elements in the shaded area.

Intersection (∩)

The intersection of sets consists of the elements *common* to those sets. Consider $A = \{1,2,3,4,5\}$ and $B = \{2,4,6\}$; then $A \cap B = \{2,4\}$.

In diagram form this can be represented as:

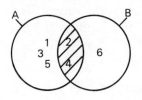

i.e. The intersection set consists of the elements in the shaded area.

The intersection set could be an empty set.

e.g. $C = \{2,4,6\}$ and $D = \{1,3,5\}$, then $C \cap D = \emptyset$ or { }.

In diagram form this can be represented as:

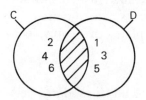

$C \cap D = \emptyset$ or { }

The Complement

If $\mathscr{E} = \{1,2,3,4,5,6,7,8\}$ and $A = \{2,4,6,8\}$, then the complement of A (A′) will consist of those elements of $\mathscr{E}$ which are *not* members of A, i.e. $A' = \{1,3,5,7\}$.

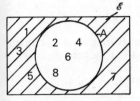

A' is the set of elements
in the shaded area.

The complement A' is the 'difference set' between the universal set $\mathscr{E}$ and the subset A.

Venn Diagrams

Diagrams are extremely useful in illustrating sets and there is a conventional method known as 'Venn diagrams'. A rectangle usually denotes the universal set and closed curves denote the subsets.

The following are useful diagrams to remember.

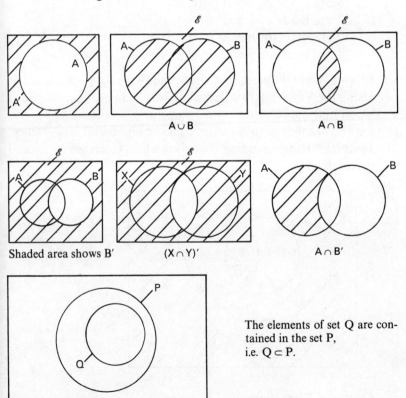

The elements of set Q are contained in the set P,
i.e. $Q \subset P$.

29

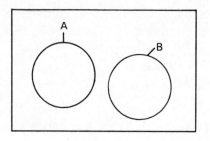

A and B are known as disjoint sets, since they have no common elements,
i.e. $A \cap B = \varnothing$ or $\{\ \}$.

A typical problem involving a Venn diagram would be:

60 toys are made of plastic (P), wood (W), metal (M), or a combination of any *two* of these materials (i.e. there is no toy made of plastic, wood and metal).

The following information is given:

       8 toys are made of plastic and wood
    15 are made of wood only
    32 are made of wood
    30 are made of metal
    24 are made of plastic

(i) Draw a Venn diagram and shade the two empty subsets of $\mathscr{E}$.

(ii) Using the Venn diagram, calculate how many toys are made of wood and metal.

(iii) Let the number of toys made of plastic and metal be x. Hence, complete the remaining two subsets in terms of x and calculate x.

(i)

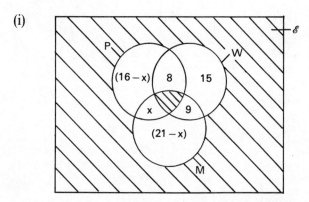

(ii) From the Venn diagram 9 toys are made of wood and metal.

(iii) If the number of toys made of plastic and metal = x, then the number of toys made of plastic only = $24 - (8 + x) = (16 - x)$; and the number of toys made of metal only = $30 - (9 + x) = (21 - x)$.

Since there are 60 toys made altogether then:

$$x + (16 - x) + 8 + 15 + 9 + (21 - x) = 60$$
$$69 - x = 60$$
$$69 - 60 = x$$
$$9 = x.$$

∴ 9 toys are made of plastic and metal; 7 toys are made of plastic only and 12 toys are made of metal only.

Particular attention should be paid to the following metric weights and measures.

Length: 10 millimetres mm = 1 centimetre cm
                       100 centimetres cm = 1 metre m
                       1000 metres m   = 1 kilometre km

Weight: 1000 grams g   = 1 kilogram kg
                       1000 kilograms kg   = 1 tonne

Remember 'kilo' means '1000'.

Capacity: 1000 cubic centimetres cm^3 = 1 litre l

Current British units to be known as well.

ALGEBRA

Algebra is an extension of Arithmetic. The same basic rules apply but in Algebra letters and symbols are used as well as numbers to represent quantities.

Addition and Subtraction

When adding and subtracting in Algebra 'like' and 'unlike' terms must be recognised. For example:

$9x + 5x$ are like terms and can be added together as $14x$.

$5p + 7q$ are unlike terms and cannot be added together. Therefore the expression must remain as $5p + 7q$.

Also $10a - 3a = 7a$, but $10a - 3b$ cannot be simplified.

e.g. Simplify $4x - 6y - 2x + x + 2y$.

Gather together like terms: $4x + x - 2x - 6y + 2y$

$$= 3x - 4y.$$

Multiplication

Avoid using the multiplication sign wherever possible in Algebra because it can be confused with the letter 'x'.

$x \times y$ is written as xy

and

$x \times x$ is written as x^2

$\therefore \; 3 \times x \times x \times y = 3x^2y$

Division

'a' divided by 'b' is written as $\dfrac{a}{b}$, and fractions in Algebra can be cancelled down in the same way as fractions in Arithmetic.

e.g. $\dfrac{\overset{2}{4}xy^{1}}{\underset{1}{2}\underset{1}{y}z} = \dfrac{2x}{z}$

Brackets

The use of brackets is a convenient way of grouping terms together. When the brackets are removed, *each term* inside the brackets is multiplied by the quantity outside the brackets.

e.g. $3(3) = 9$; $6(x) = 6x$; $5(p + 3q) = 5p + 15q$

The Expression of a Relationship in Algebraic Terms

The following examples show how verbal statements can be translated into algebraic terms.

The sum of two numbers x and y is divided by a third number z. This becomes:

$$\frac{(x + y)}{z}.$$

If 3 is added to a number and the result multiplied by 2, the answer is 18. Let the number be 'x' and the statement then becomes:

$$2(x + 3) = 18.$$

Substitution

Given the values of the letters in an algebraic expression, it is possible to find the numerical value of that expression by substitution.

e.g. If $x = 3$, $y = 4$ and $z = 5$, evaluate $\dfrac{3y + 2z}{x + z}$.

$$\frac{3y + 2z}{x + z} = \frac{3(4) + 2(5)}{3 + 5} = \frac{12 + 10}{8} = \frac{22}{8} = \frac{11}{4} = 2\tfrac{3}{4}.$$

Indices or Powers

When terms are multiplied by themselves they are written in shorthand using indices.

e.g. $x \times x \times x = x^3$; $a \times a \times a \times a = a^4$ etc.

The Rules of Indices

$x^2 \times x^3 = (x \times x) \times (x \times x \times x) = x^5$, which is the same as writing $x^2 \times x^3 = x^{2+3} = x^5$.

Rule 1. When multiplying *add* the indices.

e.g. $4y^4 \times 3y^3 = 12y^{4+3} = 12y^7$.

Rule 2. When dividing *subtract* the indices.

$$y^4 \div y^3 = \frac{\cancel{y}^1 \times \cancel{y}^1 \times \cancel{y}^1 \times y}{\cancel{y}_1 \times \cancel{y}_1 \times \cancel{y}_1} = y, \text{ which is the same as writing}$$

$$y^4 \div y^3 = y^{4-3} = y$$

Similarly $15x^5 \div 3x^2 = 5x^{5-2} = 5x^3$.

Rule 3. When raising a power to a power *multiply* the indices.

$$(x^2)^4 = x^{2 \times 4} = x^8$$

since $(x \times x) \times (x \times x) \times (x \times x) \times (x \times x)$

$$= x^8$$

Similarly $(4x^2)^3 = 64x^{2 \times 3} = 64x^6$.

Rule 4. To find a root *divide* the index by the root.

$$\sqrt[3]{x^6} = x^{6 \div 3} = x^2.$$

You can check this by cubing the answer.

i.e. $\quad (x^2)^3 = x^6$

Similarly $\quad \sqrt[4]{81x^{12}} = 3x^{12 \div 4} = 3x^3$.

Negative Indices Consider the example $x^2 \div x^5$. This can be done in two ways:

$$x^2 \div x^5 = \frac{x^2}{x^5} = \frac{1}{x^3}$$

or using Rule 2

$$x^2 \div x^5 = x^{2-5} = x^{-3}.$$

Since it is the same question then the answers must be equal,

i.e. $\quad x^{-3} = \frac{1}{x^3}.$

In other words a minus sign in front of an index means the reciprocal of that quantity (or 1 divided by the quantity).

e.g. $\quad x^{-5} = \frac{1}{x^5} \quad$ and $\quad 2^{-3} = \frac{1}{2^3} = \frac{1}{8}.$

Fractional Indices
What does $x^{1/3}$ mean? Since $x^{1/3} \times x^{1/3} \times x^{1/3} = x^{1/3 + 1/3 + 1/3} = x^1$ using Rule 1, then $x^{1/3}$ must be the cube root of x.

i.e.　　$x^{1/3} = \sqrt[3]{x}$, and $x^{1/5} = \sqrt[5]{x}$.

Also since $x^{4/3}$ means the same as $(x^{1/3})^4$ or $(x^4)^{1/3}$, then $x^{4/3}$ can be written as $\sqrt[3]{x^4}$.

Also $x^{-2/3} = \dfrac{1}{\sqrt[3]{x^2}}$　and　$8^{-2/3} = \dfrac{1}{\sqrt[3]{8^2}} = \dfrac{1}{2^2} = \dfrac{1}{4}$.

The Zero Index　　Consider the example $x^5 \div x^5$. This can be done in two ways:

$$x^5 \div x^5 = \frac{x^5}{x^5} = 1$$

or using Rule 2

$$x^5 \div x^5 = x^{5-5} = x^0.$$

Since the question is the same, the answers must be equal, i.e. $x^0 = 1$. This means that anything to the power zero equals *one*.

i.e.　　$y^0 = 1$;　$(21)^0 = 1$;　$(2p)^0 = 1$;

but　　$2p^0 = 2 \times p^0 = 2 \times 1 = 2$ (take care).

Signs
Since positive and negative terms are dealt with in Algebra, remember the simple rules for dealing with signs.

When adding terms with the same signs, add the terms and the sign of the sum will be the same as the signs of the terms.

e.g.　　$4y + 2y + 3y = +9y$　or　$-4y - 2y - 3y = -9y$.

When subtracting a term, change its sign and add the resulting term.

e.g.　　$10p - (-4p) = 10p + 4p = 14p$.

Also　　$5 - (+7) = 5 - 7 = -2$

or　　$6a - (2a + 3) = 6a - 2a - 3 = 4a - 3$.

When multiplying or dividing terms with *like* signs, the answer is

35

always positive. When multiplying or dividing terms with *unlike* signs, the answer is always negative.

e.g.

$$(+4b) \times (+3b) = +12b^2 \qquad (+12rs) \div (+4s) = +3r$$

$$(-4b) \times (-3b) = +12b^2 \qquad (-12rs) \div (-4s) = +3r$$

$$(+4b) \times (-3b) = -12b^2 \qquad (-12rs) \div (+4s) = -3r$$

$$(-4b) \times (+3b) = -12b^2 \qquad (+12rs) \div (-4s) = -3r$$

Expansion of Brackets
Remember the rules for signs.

$$2(y+3) = 2y+6 \quad ; \quad -2(y+3) = -2y-6$$

$$-2(y-3) = -2y+6 \quad ; \quad 2(y-3) = 2y-6$$

When there are two sets of brackets to expand, each term in the second bracket is multiplied by each term in the first bracket, and the resulting expression is then simplified.

$$(x+2)(x+3) = x^2 + 3x + 2x + 6$$
$$= x^2 + 5x + 6 \quad ;$$
$$(x-2)(x-3) = x^2 - 3x - 2x + 6$$
$$= x^2 - 5x + 6$$
$$(x+2)(x-3) = x^2 - 3x + 2x - 6$$
$$= x^2 - x - 6 \quad ;$$
$$(x-2)(x+3) = x^2 + 3x - 2x - 6$$
$$= x^2 + x - 6.$$

Factorisation
This is the reverse of the expansion of brackets. It means writing an algebraic expression as a product of two or more terms or expressions. Find the factor common to all the terms first. The second factor is then found by dividing the expression by this common factor.

$$3y + 9 = 3(y+3) \quad ; \quad \text{3 is common to both 3y and 9.}$$

$$mx - my + mz = m(x - y + z) \quad ; \quad \text{m is common to mx, my}$$
and mz.

36

$3p(x-y)-q(x-y)=(x-y)(3p-q)$; this time $(x-y)$ is the common factor.

Factors by Grouping

$2x^2+3ax+2xy+3ay$

Where there is no factor common to all the terms, group the terms that do possess a common factor.

$(2x^2+2xy)+(3ax+3ay)$

$2x(x+y)+3a(x+y)$

Having now made *two* terms instead of four, factorise each term. There is now a factor common to both terms, namely $(x+y)$.

$\therefore$ The factors of the original expression are $(x+y)(2x+3a)$.

Be careful when separating a minus sign from its term by a bracket. Remember the question is being rewritten; *it must not be changed.* If the brackets are removed, the original expression should be restored.

e.g. $4ay+by-4az-bz$

minus sign $\downarrow$ so this sign becomes plus $\downarrow$

Step 1.   Group terms $(4ay+by)-(4az+bz)$

Step 2.   Factorise each term $y(4a+b)-z(4a+b)$

Step 3.   Take out the common factor $(4a+b)(y-z)$.

Factorisation of Trinomials

Step 1.   Look at the sign of the last term. If this is *plus*, the signs in the brackets will be the same and factors of the first and last terms are needed which will *add* to give the middle term. If it is *minus*, the signs in the brackets will be different and factors of the first and last terms are needed which will subtract to give the middle term.

Step 2.   Choose the appropriate factors of the first and last terms.

Step 3.   If the signs in the brackets are to be the same, the sign of the middle term will tell *what* they are. If the signs are to be different, the sign of the middle term will tell *where* to put the plus and the minus.

e.g. 6×1 40×1 $6x^2+31x+40$

Sign *plus*, so signs in brackets will be the same.

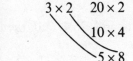 $(3x+8)(2x+5)$

Middle term is positive; thus the signs in the brackets are both plus signs.

$9 \times 1 \qquad 4 \times 1 \qquad 9x^2 - 12x + 4$ — Sign plus, so signs in brackets will be the same.

$3 \times 3 \underline{\quad} 2 \times 2 \qquad (3x - 2)(3x - 2)$ — Middle term is negative; thus the signs in the brackets are both minus signs.

$10 \times 1 \qquad 15 \times 1 \qquad 10a^2 + 19a - 15$ — Sign *minus*, so signs in brackets will be different.

Since it is necessary to end up with $+19a$, there must be more pluses than minuses.

$5 \times 2 \qquad 5 \times 3 \qquad (5a - 3)(2a + 5)$

$4 \times 1 \qquad 6 \times 1 \qquad 4x^2 - 10x - 6$ — Sign minus, so signs in brackets will be different.

Since it is necessary to end up with $-10x$, there must be more minuses than pluses.

$2 \times 2 \qquad 3 \times 2 \qquad (4x + 2)(x - 3)$

Difference of Two Squares

This type of expression is easy to recognise since each term will be a perfect square and connected by a minus sign, e.g. $x^2 - y^2$.

The factors will consist of the square root of each term, added in one bracket and subtracted in the other.

Example 1.   Example 2.

$$x^2 - y^2 = (x + y)(x - y) \qquad 4x^2 - 9y^2 = (2x + 3y)(2x - 3y)$$

Example 3.

$$4(2x + 3y)^2 - 9(x + 2y)^2$$
$$= \left[2(2x + 3y) + 3(x + 2y)\right]\left[2(2x + 3y) - 3(x + 2y)\right]$$

These factors can then be simplified.

This method is often useful in Arithmetic when asked to evaluate expressions such as $(73.6)^2 - (26.4)^2$. It should be recognised as a difference of two squares and therefore can be written as:

$$(73.6 + 26.4)(73.6 - 26.4)$$
$$= (100)(47.2)$$
$$= 4720.$$

This is much easier than squaring 73.6 and 26.4 and then subtracting one answer from the other.

Special Expansions

It is worth while learning these because if the pattern is recognised it can save time in expansion of brackets or factorisation.

Perfect Squares always follow one of the following patterns.

$$(A+B)^2 = A^2 + 2AB + B^2 \quad or \quad (A-B)^2 = A^2 - 2AB + B^2$$

Difference of Two Squares:

$$(A+B)(A-B) = A^2 - B^2.$$

Equations

Always remember an equation is like a see-saw which is balanced ‾△‾, or a set of scales in a position of balance ⌐ △ ⌐.

An equation can be altered in any number of ways provided the balance is not upset. This means doing the same thing to each side of the equation. To solve an equation means to find the value of the unknown quantity.

Example 1. $\quad x + 6 = 12$

$\qquad x + 6 - 6 = 12 - 6$

** $\qquad x = 12 - 6$

$\qquad x = 6$

Example 2. $\quad x - 6 = 12$

$\qquad x - 6 + 6 = 12 + 6$

** $\qquad x = 12 + 6$

$\qquad x = 18$

Example 3. $\quad 3x = 12$

$\qquad \dfrac{3x}{3} = \dfrac{12}{3}$

** $\qquad x = \dfrac{12}{3}$

$\qquad x = 4$

Example 4. $\quad \dfrac{x}{3} = 4$

$\qquad \dfrac{x}{3} \times 3 = 4 \times 3$

** $\qquad x = 4 \times 3$

$\qquad x = 12$

A simple rule emerges from these four examples. In example 1 it was necessary to get rid of $+6$, and in so doing the ** line ended up with -6 on the other side. In example 2, to get rid of -6, the ** line ended up with $+6$ on the other side. In example 3, multiplying x by 3 meant dividing by 3 on the other side of the ** line. In example 4, dividing x by 3 meant multiplying by 3 on the other side of the ** line.

The rule is: *Whatever is got rid of on one side of an equation, exactly the opposite must be done with that quantity on the other side of the equation.*

Of course most equations require several applications of this rule plus the basic rules of simplification.

e.g.
$$4(x-5) = 7-5(3-2x)$$
$$4x-20 = 7-15+10x$$
$$4x-20 = -8+10x$$

Remove the brackets and simplify where possible.

$$-20+8 = 10x-4x$$
$$-12 = 6x$$
$$\frac{-12}{6} = x$$
$$-2 = x$$

Isolate the unknown quantity using the above rule.

Quadratic Equations

These must be treated differently. To isolate the unknown quantity it is necessary to get *all* the terms to one side of the equation leaving *zero* on the other side and then factorise. There will be *two* possible solutions.

Example 1. $x^2 + 6x - 16 = 0$

$$(x+8)(x-2) = 0$$

∴ Either $x+8=0$ *or* $x-2=0$ ←——

Since the product can be zero only if at least one of the terms in the product is zero.

and $x = -8$ *or* $x = 2$.

Example 2. $2x^2 + 6 = 7x$

$$2x^2 - 7x + 6 = 0$$

$$(2x-3)(x-2) = 0$$

∴ Either $2x-3=0$ *or* $x-2=0$

and $2x = 3$ *or* $x = 2$

   $x = 1\frac{1}{2}$

40

L.C.M. of Algebraic Expressions

To find the L.C.M. of algebraic expressions first *factorise* the expressions.

Example 1. Find the L.C.M. of $3x - 6$ and $x^2 - 5x + 6$.

$\quad$ Factorise $\longrightarrow 3(x-2) \quad ; \quad (x-2)(x-3)$

$\therefore \quad$ L.C.M. $= 3(x-2)(x-3)$.

Example 2. Find the L.C.M. of $x^2 - 4x + 4$ and $x^2 + 2x - 8$.

$\quad$ Factorise $\longrightarrow (x-2)^2 \quad ; \quad (x-2)(x+4)$

$\therefore \quad$ L.C.M. $= (x-2)^2(x+4)$.

Fractions

The rules are as for fractions in Arithmetic.

Example 1. $\dfrac{4}{x+2} - \dfrac{2}{x-3}$

$$\text{L.C.M.} \rightarrow \; = \frac{4(x-3) - 2(x+2)}{(x+2)(x-3)} \leftarrow \text{Watch signs.}$$

$$= \frac{4x - 12 - 2x - 4}{(x+2)(x-3)}$$

$$= \frac{2x - 16}{(x+2)(x-3)}$$

$$= \frac{2(x-8)}{(x+2)(x-3)}$$

Example 2. $\dfrac{6ab}{5cd} \div \dfrac{4a^2}{7bd}$

$$= \frac{\cancel{6}^{3}a b}{5c\cancel{d}_{1}} \times \frac{7b\cancel{d}^{1}}{\cancel{4}_{2} \, \cancel{a^2}_{a}}$$

$$= \frac{21b^2}{10ac}$$

Fractional Equations

There are two methods of solving fractional equations depending on the type of denominator present. Method 2 is dealt with on page 68.

Method 1

This method should be used whenever the denominators are numbers only or very simple algebraic expressions such as y, 2y, etc.

$\quad$ The method involves getting rid of all the denominators at the same time by multiplying the whole equation by the L.C.M. of the denominators.

e.g.
$$\frac{4x-3}{3} = \frac{3x-1}{2} - \frac{2}{3}$$

Multiply through by 6.

$$\frac{\overset{2}{\cancel{6}}(4x-3)}{\cancel{3}_1} = \frac{\overset{3}{\cancel{6}}(3x-1)}{\cancel{2}_1} - \frac{\overset{2}{\cancel{6}}(2)}{\cancel{3}_1}$$

$$2(4x-3) = 3(3x-1)-4$$

$$8x-6 = 9x-3-4$$

$$8x-6 = 9x-7$$

$$-6+7 = 9x-8x$$

$$1 = x$$

Simultaneous Equations

If there are two unknowns, two equations are needed and, by arranging if necessary that there is the same quantity of one of the unknowns in both equations, this unknown can be eliminated by adding or subtracting the equations and the second unknown can then be found by substitution.

e.g.
$$x + 3y = 7 \dots ①$$
$$2x - 2y = 6 \dots ②$$

Multiply ① by 2.

$$2x + 6y = 14 \dots ③$$
$$2x - 2y = \;\;6 \dots ②$$

Subtract ② from ③. $8y = 8$

Watch·signs. $y = 1$

Substitute in ① for 'y'.   Check

$$x + 3y = 7 \qquad\qquad x + 3y = 7$$
$$x + 3 = 7 \qquad\qquad 4 + 3 = 7$$
$$x = 7-3 = 4 \qquad\qquad 7 = 7.$$

$$\left.\begin{array}{l} \therefore\; x = 4 \\ y = 1 \end{array}\right\}$$

42

Literal Equations

These are equations or formulae involving several letters, and using the basic principle for the solution of equations, they can be rearranged to express any one of the letters in terms of the others.

There are a number of ways in which the questions can be asked:

'Make "x" the subject of the following ...' or 'Find "y" in terms of "x" and "z" in the following equation ...' or 'Rearrange the following formula to find "p" ...' etc.

e.g. Make q the subject of the formula $p = \sqrt{\dfrac{q+x}{q-y}}$.

$$p = \sqrt{\frac{q+x}{q-y}}$$

$$p^2 = \frac{q+x}{q-y}$$

$$p^2q - p^2y = q + x$$

Factorise to isolate q. $\quad p^2q - q = p^2y + x$

$$q(p^2 - 1) = p^2y + x$$

$$q = \frac{p^2y + x}{(p^2 - 1)}$$

Problems Many problems can be solved more easily by building up equations with the relevant data and then, depending on the type of equation or equations formed, solving them by the most appropriate of the methods listed.

Matrices

People like to have information at their fingertips and so have become well used to tables which make all kinds of information readily available. A matrix is simply a table in the form of an array of numbers.

e.g. Three hampers containing four types of fruit are offered for sale. The following table shows the number of each type of fruit contained in the different hampers.

Type	Apples	Oranges	Pears	Bananas
A	4	3	2	2
B	5	6	4	3
C	3	4	3	0

If the headings are left out and the numbers presented are enclosed in a bracket, the table is said to be in matrix form:

$$\begin{pmatrix} 4 & 3 & 2 & 2 \\ 5 & 6 & 4 & 3 \\ 3 & 4 & 3 & 0 \end{pmatrix}$$

Since there are 3 rows and 4 columns it is called a 3×4 matrix.

Types of Matrices
A matrix with only one row is said to be a *row matrix*,

e.g. $(4 \quad 7)$.

Likewise, a matrix with only one column is said to be a *column matrix*,

e.g. $\begin{pmatrix} 3 \\ 2 \end{pmatrix}$.

A matrix with all its elements zero is known as a *null matrix*,

e.g. $\begin{pmatrix} 0 & 0 \\ 0 & 0 \end{pmatrix}$.

If a matrix has the same number of rows and columns it is called a *square matrix*,

e.g. $\begin{pmatrix} 1 & 5 \\ 4 & 6 \end{pmatrix}$.

A square matrix with all the elements zero except the elements running diagonally from upper left to lower right is called a *diagonal matrix*,

e.g. $\begin{pmatrix} 4 & 0 \\ 0 & 7 \end{pmatrix}$.

The special diagonal matrix where the diagonal elements equal 1 is known as the *unit matrix*, e.g. $\begin{pmatrix} 1 & 0 \\ 0 & 1 \end{pmatrix}.$

Addition and Subtraction

Matrices can be added or subtracted provided they are of the same order, i.e. both 2×2 or both 3×4, etc.

To add or subtract two matrices, simply add or subtract the corresponding elements of the matrices.

Example 1.

$$\begin{pmatrix} 3 & 4 \\ -3 & 1 \end{pmatrix} + \begin{pmatrix} 1 & 2 \\ 2 & 4 \end{pmatrix} = \begin{pmatrix} 3+1 & 4+2 \\ -3+2 & 1+4 \end{pmatrix} = \begin{pmatrix} 4 & 6 \\ -1 & 5 \end{pmatrix}$$

Example 2.

$$\begin{pmatrix} 6 & 2 \\ 3 & 8 \end{pmatrix} - \begin{pmatrix} 5 & 4 \\ -1 & 3 \end{pmatrix} = \begin{pmatrix} 6-5 & 2-4 \\ 3-(-1) & 8-3 \end{pmatrix} = \begin{pmatrix} 1 & -2 \\ 4 & 5 \end{pmatrix}$$

Multiplication

(a) *Scalar multiplication*
To multiply a matrix by a scalar (or number), simply multiply each element of the matrix by that scalar.

e.g. $3\begin{pmatrix} 1 & 4 \\ 0 & 2 \end{pmatrix} = \begin{pmatrix} 3 \times 1 & 3 \times 4 \\ 3 \times 0 & 3 \times 2 \end{pmatrix} = \begin{pmatrix} 3 & 12 \\ 0 & 6 \end{pmatrix}$

(b) *General matrix multiplication*
The multiplication is done by multiplying a row by a column as shown in the example following. Therefore two matrices can be multiplied only if the number of rows in the one is equal to the number of columns in the other.

Example 1.

$$\begin{pmatrix} 2 & 3 \\ 1 & 8 \end{pmatrix} \times \begin{pmatrix} 3 & 4 \\ 2 & 5 \end{pmatrix} = \begin{pmatrix} 2 \times 3 + 3 \times 2 & 2 \times 4 + 3 \times 5 \\ 1 \times 3 + 8 \times 2 & 1 \times 4 + 8 \times 5 \end{pmatrix}$$

$$= \begin{pmatrix} 12 & 23 \\ 19 & 44 \end{pmatrix}$$

Example 2.

$$\begin{pmatrix} 3 & 1 \\ 2 & 4 \end{pmatrix} \times \begin{pmatrix} 6 \\ 7 \end{pmatrix} = \begin{pmatrix} 3 \times 6 + 1 \times 7 \\ 2 \times 6 + 4 \times 7 \end{pmatrix} = \begin{pmatrix} 25 \\ 40 \end{pmatrix}$$

45

N.B. With certain exceptions, multiplication of matrices is *not* commutative.

i.e. $A.B \neq B.A$

Scalar Division

Division by a scalar should be thought of as multiplication by the reciprocal of the scalar, i.e. to divide by 4 means to multiply by $\frac{1}{4}$.

e.g. $\frac{1}{4}\begin{pmatrix} 4 & 36 \\ 12 & 16 \end{pmatrix} = \begin{pmatrix} 1 & 9 \\ 3 & 4 \end{pmatrix}$

Application of Matrices

Costing problem   A firm makes two types of bicycle, type A and type B, at two of its factories. Factory I works 6 days a week and Factory II works 5 days a week. The average number of bicycles made per day is shown in the table below. On average, how many bicycles are made per week?

	Type A	Type B
Factory I	40	35
Factory II	34	20

If type A sells for £90 and type B sells for £74, find the value of the bicycles made in a week.

(a) No. of bicycles made per week:

$$(6 \quad 5)\begin{pmatrix} 40 & 35 \\ 34 & 20 \end{pmatrix} = (240+170 \quad 210+100)$$

$$= (410 \quad 310) = 720 \text{ bicycles.}$$

(b) Value of bicycles made per week:

$$(410 \quad 310)\begin{pmatrix} 90 \\ 74 \end{pmatrix} = (410 \times 90 + 310 \times 74)$$

$$= (36\,900 + 22\,940) = £59\,840.$$

Transformations

A column matrix can be used to represent the co-ordinates of a point on a graph. If such a point is given a new position it is said to have undergone a transformation. If a line takes up a new position, then every point on that line has moved the same distance in the same direction and the line is said to have been translated.

Consideration of what happens to the *unit* matrix under various transformations will produce matrices that can be used to find out what happens to other points under the same transformations.

Reflections

(a) *Reflection in the 'x' axis.*
The points of the unit matrix $\begin{pmatrix} 1 & 0 \\ 0 & 1 \end{pmatrix}$ have been plotted on the axes in the diagram. After reflection in the 'x' axis the result is $\begin{pmatrix} 1 & 0 \\ 0 & -1 \end{pmatrix}$.

The point $\begin{pmatrix} 1 \\ 0 \end{pmatrix}$ remains unaltered but the point $\begin{pmatrix} 0 \\ 1 \end{pmatrix}$ becomes $\begin{pmatrix} 0 \\ -1 \end{pmatrix}$.

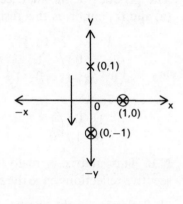

e.g. Find the images A′, B′ and C′ of the points A, B and C after reflection in the 'x' axis, given that the co-ordinates of A, B and C are (2,3), (5,2) and (4,5) respectively.

$$\begin{pmatrix} 1 & 0 \\ 0 & -1 \end{pmatrix}\begin{pmatrix} 2 \\ 3 \end{pmatrix} = \begin{pmatrix} 2 \\ -3 \end{pmatrix} \quad ; \quad \begin{pmatrix} 1 & 0 \\ 0 & -1 \end{pmatrix}\begin{pmatrix} 5 \\ 2 \end{pmatrix} = \begin{pmatrix} 5 \\ -2 \end{pmatrix} \quad ;$$

$$\begin{pmatrix} 1 & 0 \\ 0 & -1 \end{pmatrix}\begin{pmatrix} 4 \\ 5 \end{pmatrix} = \begin{pmatrix} 4 \\ -5 \end{pmatrix}$$

Therefore the co-ordinates of A′, B′ and C′ are $(2,-3)$, $(5,-2)$ and $(4,-5)$ respectively.

In the same way we can find matrices to represent other transformations as follows:

(b) *Reflection in the 'y' axis*
Under this transformation the unit matrix becomes

$$\begin{pmatrix} -1 & 0 \\ 0 & 1 \end{pmatrix}.$$

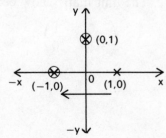

47

(c) *Reflection in the 'x' and then the 'y' axes or vice versa*
Under this transformation the unit
matrix becomes

$$\begin{pmatrix} -1 & 0 \\ 0 & -1 \end{pmatrix}.$$

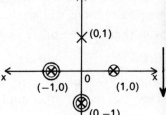

The product of the matrices in
(a) and (b) confirms this result.

$$\begin{array}{cc} \text{In 'x'} & \text{In 'y'} \\ \begin{pmatrix} 1 & 0 \\ 0 & -1 \end{pmatrix} \begin{pmatrix} -1 & 0 \\ 0 & 1 \end{pmatrix} = \begin{pmatrix} -1 & 0 \\ 0 & -1 \end{pmatrix} \end{array}$$

$$\begin{array}{cc} \text{In 'y'} & \text{In 'x'} \\ or \quad \begin{pmatrix} -1 & 0 \\ 0 & 1 \end{pmatrix} \begin{pmatrix} 1 & 0 \\ 0 & -1 \end{pmatrix} = \begin{pmatrix} -1 & 0 \\ 0 & -1 \end{pmatrix} \end{array}$$

N.B. This matrix is really a rotational matrix since two consecutive reflections have the same effect as a rotation through 180°.

(d) *Reflection in the line through the origin at 45° to the 'x' axis*
(i.e. the y = x line)
Under this transformation
the unit matrix becomes

$$\begin{pmatrix} 0 & 1 \\ 1 & 0 \end{pmatrix}.$$

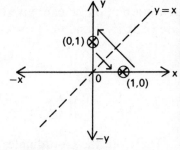

(e) *Reflection in the line through the origin at 135° to the 'x' axis*
(i.e. the y = −x line)
The unit matrix now becomes

$$\begin{pmatrix} 0 & -1 \\ -1 & 0 \end{pmatrix}.$$

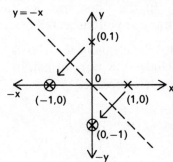

Rotations

(a) *Rotation of 90° clockwise about the origin*

The unit matrix becomes $\begin{pmatrix} 0 & 1 \\ -1 & 0 \end{pmatrix}$.

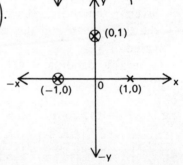

Two consecutive rotations of 90° are the same as one rotation of 180° and, as we have already discovered in part (c) on Reflections, the matrix representing this transformation is $\begin{pmatrix} -1 & 0 \\ 0 & -1 \end{pmatrix}$.

We can check this now by considering two rotations of 90°:

$$\begin{pmatrix} 0 & 1 \\ -1 & 0 \end{pmatrix}\begin{pmatrix} 0 & 1 \\ -1 & 0 \end{pmatrix} = \begin{pmatrix} -1 & 0 \\ 0 & -1 \end{pmatrix}.$$

(b) *Rotation of 90° anticlockwise*

The unit matrix becomes $\begin{pmatrix} 0 & -1 \\ 1 & 0 \end{pmatrix}$.

N.B. two consecutive anticlockwise rotations of 90° are the same as one anticlockwise (or clockwise) rotation of 180°.

Enlargements

The matrix representing an enlargement is of the form $\begin{pmatrix} k & 0 \\ 0 & k \end{pmatrix}$ where $k > 0$.

e.g. Enlarge triangle ABC by a factor of 3 if the co-ordinates of A, B and C are (1,2), (2,3) and (3,1) respectively.

$$\begin{pmatrix} 3 & 0 \\ 0 & 3 \end{pmatrix}\begin{pmatrix} 1 \\ 2 \end{pmatrix} = \begin{pmatrix} 3 \\ 6 \end{pmatrix} \quad ; \quad \begin{pmatrix} 3 & 0 \\ 0 & 3 \end{pmatrix}\begin{pmatrix} 2 \\ 3 \end{pmatrix} = \begin{pmatrix} 6 \\ 9 \end{pmatrix} \quad ;$$

$$\begin{pmatrix} 3 & 0 \\ 0 & 3 \end{pmatrix}\begin{pmatrix} 3 \\ 1 \end{pmatrix} = \begin{pmatrix} 9 \\ 3 \end{pmatrix}$$

The co-ordinates of A′, B′ and C′ are (3,6), (6,9) and (9,3) respectively.

Graphs

A graph is a pictorial representation of mathematical data.

Candidates are expected to construct and interpret charts and graphs including conversion graphs and travel graphs.

In this section the emphasis is on the mechanics of plotting simple conversion graphs, travel graphs and straight line graphs from algebraic equations.

Bar charts, Pie charts, Histograms, etc., are dealt with separately under the heading of Statistics in PART TWO.

Points to Remember

1. Graphs are plotted against two axes: the horizontal or 'x' axis and the vertical or 'y' axis. The horizontal and vertical axes can represent anything required: Distance/Time; Kilometres/Miles; Inches of rainfall/Months of the year, etc.

2. Points on the graph are fixed by co-ordinates which are usually given in the form (2,3), where the first number (2 in this case) is the value of 'x' and the second number (3 in this case) is the value of 'y'.

Generally, candidates will be required to work out the co-ordinates themselves using a given rule and certain starting values of 'x'.

e.g.   Plot the co-ordinates A(2,3); B(−1,2); and C(2,−1).

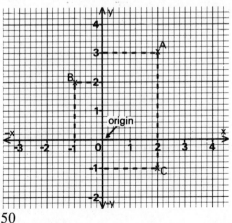

Always mark the plotted points with a cross. Always arrow and label the axes.

Conversion Graphs

e.g.

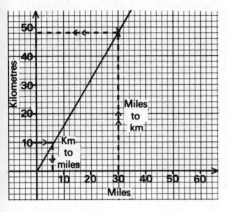

To convert miles to kilo-metres, choose the required number of miles on the horizontal axis and move vertically until the line of the graph is reached; then move horizontally to the vertical axis and read off your answer. To convert kilo-metres to miles, simply reverse the process.

Straight Line Graphs always follow the general pattern $y = mx + c$.

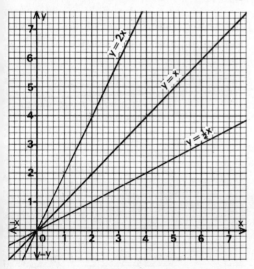

The above graphs show that the coefficient of the 'x' term affects the slope of the line.

This means that 'm' in the general equation $y = mx + c$ represents the slope of the graph. The sign of this coefficient will also indicate whether the slope of the graph is positive or negative.

51

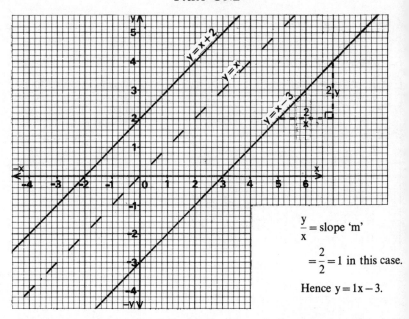

$$\frac{y}{x} = \text{slope 'm'}$$

$$= \frac{2}{2} = 1 \text{ in this case.}$$

Hence $y = 1x - 3$.

The above graphs show that adding a constant term has the effect of moving the graph a number of units up or down in the 'y' direction.

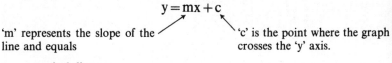

$$y = mx + c$$

'm' represents the slope of the line and equals

'c' is the point where the graph crosses the 'y' axis.

$$\frac{y}{x} \text{ or } \frac{\text{vertical distance}}{\text{horizontal distance}}.$$

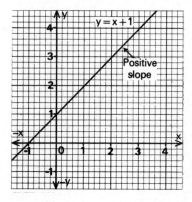

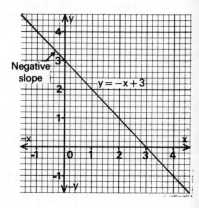

If two graphs intersect, then at the point of intersection they are equal. This provides a graphical method of solving simultaneous equations. The co-ordinates of the point of intersection give the solutions of the equations.

e.g. Solve the following simultaneous equations graphically: $y = x + 2$ and $3x - y = 2$.

Plot the graphs $y = x + 2$ and $y = 3x - 2$ on the same axes.

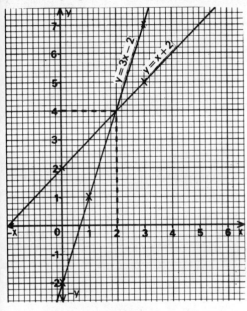

The co-ordinates of the point of intersection are (2,4).

$\therefore$ The solutions of the equations are $\left.\begin{array}{l} x = 2 \\ y = 4 \end{array}\right\}$.

Distance/Time Graphs

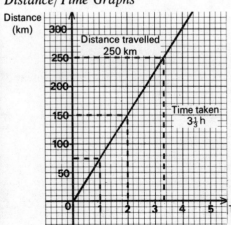

$\text{Slope} = \dfrac{75 \ \text{(vert.)}}{1 \ \text{(horiz.)}}$

On a distance/time graph the slope represents speed.

The speed shown above
$= 75$ km/h.

53

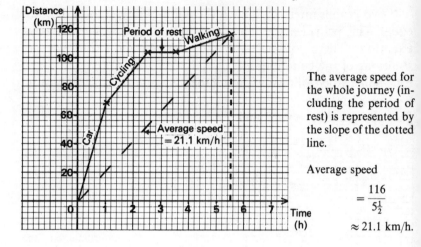

The average speed for the whole journey (including the period of rest) is represented by the slope of the dotted line.

Average speed

$$= \frac{116}{5\frac{1}{2}}$$

$$\approx 21.1 \text{ km/h}.$$

Inequalities

Quantities are often said to be greater than or less than other quantities, e.g. 8 is greater than 3, or 4 centimetres is less than 5 metres.

Such statements are called *inequalities*. Solutions of simple inequalities can be found by a process similar to that of solving simple equations.

e.g.
$$2x + 5 > 7$$
$$2x > 7 - 5$$
$$2x > 2$$
$$x > 1$$

Examples of examination questions on inequalities:

1. Given that $x + 2 \leqslant 8$ and $2x - 3 \geqslant 1$, write down the lower and upper limits of x.

$$
\begin{array}{ll}
x + 2 \leqslant 8 & 2x - 3 \geqslant 1 \\
x \leqslant 8 - 2 & 2x \geqslant 1 + 3 \\
x \leqslant 6 & 2x \geqslant 4 \\
& x \geqslant 2
\end{array}
$$

Therefore the lower limit of x is 2 and the upper limit is 6.

54

Often examination questions link inequalities and graphs as follows.

2. Draw the graph of $y = \frac{1}{2}x + 1$ and $y = -x + 3$ and shade the area where $y > 0$, $x > 0$, $y > \frac{1}{2}x + 1$ and $y < -x + 3$.

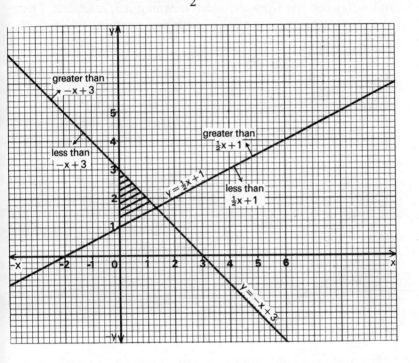

GEOMETRY

The word Geometry is made up of two parts — *geo* meaning earth and *metry* coming from the word meaning measurement. Therefore the word *geometry* means 'earth measurement'.

The Basic Rules

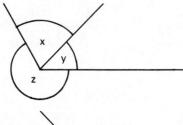

Angles at a point add up to 360°.
i.e. $x + y + z = 360°$.
'x' is an acute angle, i.e. $<90°$.
'z' is a reflex angle, i.e. $>180°$.

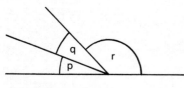

Adjacent angles on a straight line add up to 180°.
i.e. $p + q + r = 180°$.
'r' is an obtuse angle, i.e. $>90°$ but $<180°$.

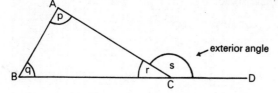

exterior angle

The angle sum of a triangle is 180°, i.e. $p + q + r = 180°$.
The exterior angle of a triangle = the sum of the two interior opposite angles, i.e. $s = p + q$.

Angle Properties of Parallel Lines

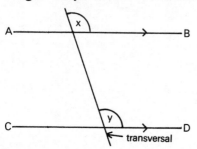

transversal

'x' and 'y' are *corresponding angles* and if the lines they rest on are *parallel* then $x = y$.

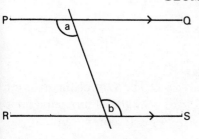

'a' and 'b' are *alternate angles* and if the lines they rest on are *parallel* then a = b.

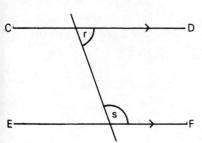

When the lines CD and EF are parallel then 'r' and 's' are known as *supplementary angles*. i.e. r + s = 180°.

Polygons

A polygon is any closed figure with three or more sides, e.g. triangles, quadrilaterals, pentagons, etc.

If a polygon is 'regular' then all its sides are equal in length and all its angles are equal.

> The sum of the interior angles of a polygon =
> (2n − 4) right angles

where 'n' is the number of sides.

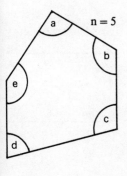

$$a+b+c+d+e = (2n-4) \text{ rt. } \angle\text{s.}$$
$$= (2 \times 5 - 4) \text{ rt. } \angle\text{s.}$$
$$= (10 - 4) \text{ rt. } \angle\text{s.}$$
$$= 6 \text{ rt. } \angle\text{s.}$$
$$= 6 \times 90°$$
$$= 540°$$

57

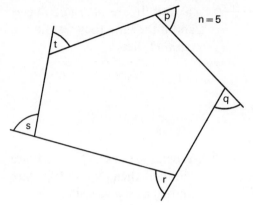

n = 5

The sum of the exterior angles of any polygon is 360°, or 4 right angles. i.e. $p+q+r+s+t=360°$. The exterior angle sum does not depend on the number of sides.

Types of Triangle

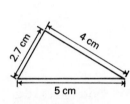

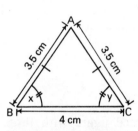

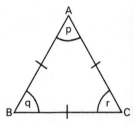

A *scalene* triangle. No equal sides; no equal angles.

An *isosceles* triangle has two equal sides and the angles opposite these sides are also equal. i.e. $AB=AC$ and $x=y$.

An *equilateral* triangle has three equal sides and three equal angles. i.e. $AB=BC=CA$ and $p=q=r=60°$.

Congruency

Triangles are congruent if they are equal in size and shape.

Four Conditions of Congruency

1. Three sides in one triangle equal to the corresponding three sides in the other.

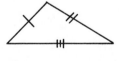

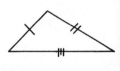

2. Two sides and the included angle in one triangle equal to the corresponding two sides and the included angle in the other.

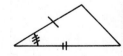

58

3. One side and two angles
   in one triangle equal to
   one side and two angles
   in the other.

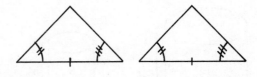

4. One side, a right angle
   and the hypotenuse in
   one triangle equal to
   the corresponding side,
   right angle and hypo-
   tenuse of the other.

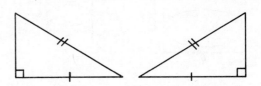

Similar Triangles

Similar triangles have the same shape (i.e. are equiangular) but are not the same size.

The ratios of corresponding sides of similar triangles are equal.

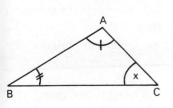
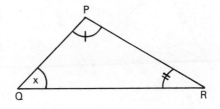

$$\frac{AB}{PR} = \frac{BC}{QR} = \frac{AC}{PQ}$$

The ratio of the areas of similar figures is equal to the ratio of the squares of any pair of corresponding sides.

i.e. $$\frac{\text{Area of } \triangle ABC}{\text{Area of } \triangle PQR} = \frac{AB^2}{PR^2} = \frac{BC^2}{QR^2} = \frac{AC^2}{PQ^2}.$$

Similar Solids

The volumes of similar solids are proportional to the cubes of their corresponding linear dimensions.

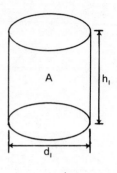
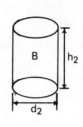

$$\frac{\text{Volume of A}}{\text{Volume of B}} = \frac{(h_1)^3}{(h_2)^3} = \frac{(d_1)^3}{(d_2)^3}$$

Properties of Special Quadrilaterals

(a) *Parallelogram*

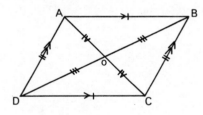

1. Opposite sides are equal and parallel.
2. Opposite angles are equal, e.g. $\angle DAB = \angle BCD$.
3. The diagonals bisect each other.
4. The diagonal bisects the area of the parallelogram.

(b) *Rectangle*

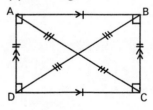

The rectangle possesses the basic four properties of the parallelogram *plus*:
5. The diagonals are equal in length.
   i.e. $AC = BD$.
   Also all its angles are 90°.

(c) *Rhombus*

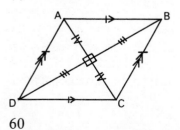

All its sides are equal.
The rhombus possesses the four properties of a parallelogram *plus*:
5. The diagonals bisect each other at right angles.

60

(d) *Square*

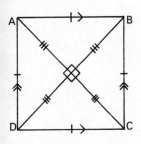

All its angles are 90° and all its sides are equal.

The square possesses the four properties of a parallelogram *plus*:

5. Its diagonals are equal in length.
6. Its diagonals bisect each other at right angles.

Pythagoras' Theorem

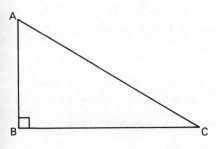

In a right-angled triangle the square on the hypotenuse equals the sum of the squares on the other two sides.

i.e. $AC^2 = AB^2 + BC^2$
Remember, the hypotenuse is the side opposite the right angle.

The Geometry of the Circle: Points to Remember

The perpendicular from the centre of a circle onto a chord bisects the chord.

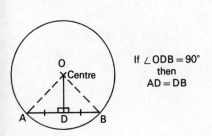

If ∠ODB = 90°
then
AD = DB

The proof is by congruency using triangles AOD and DOB.

The converse of the theorem states that the line from the centre to the mid point of a chord must be perpendicular to the chord.

61

The tangent to a circle is perpendicular to the radius at the point of contact.

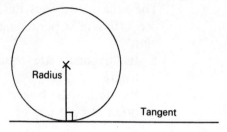

Tangents to a circle from an external point are equal.

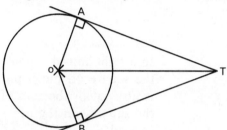

This again is easily proved by congruency using triangles AOT and BOT. AT = TB and OT bisects ∠AOB and ∠ATB.

The angle which an arc subtends at the centre is twice the angle which it subtends at any other point on the remaining part of the circumference.

'O' is the centre of the circle.
∠AOC = 2∠ABC.

Angles in the same segment of a circle are equal.

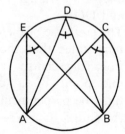

∠ACB = ∠ADB
= ∠AEB

GEOMETRY

The angle in a semicircle is a right angle.

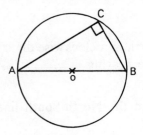

AB is a diameter.
∠ACB = 90°.

Angle properties of a cyclic quadrilateral.

(i)

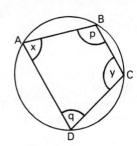

Opposite angles are supplementary.

i.e. $p + q = 180°$
and $x + y = 180°$.

(ii)

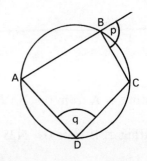

The exterior angle of a cyclic quadrilateral equals the interior opposite angle.

i.e. $p = q$.

Constructions
The following constructions should be known.

(a) Bisection of angles and lines
(b) Perpendicular to a line from a point on or outside the line
(c) Constructions of angles of 60°, 30°, 45°, 90°
(d) Parallels to a given straight line
(e) Triangles and quadrilaterals from given data

Bearings
In the horizontal plane.

True Bearings
True bearings are measured from North in a clockwise direction. *Three* digits are used in stating such a bearing.

Compass Bearings
Compass bearings are measured from the North/South line to either East or West.

e.g.

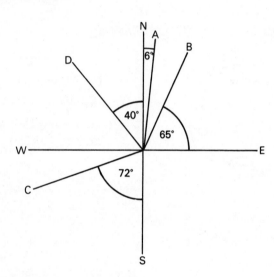

True bearing of A from 0 = 006°:
    Compass bearing of A from 0 = N6°E
True bearing of B from 0 = 025°:
    Compass bearing of B from 0 = N25°E
True bearing of C from 0 = 252°:
    Compass bearing of C from 0 = S72°W
True bearing of D from 0 = 320°:
    Compass bearing of D from 0 = N40°W

Symmetry
(a) *Symmetry about a Line*
The line is known as the axis of symmetry, and if a shape is symmetrical then it is completely balanced about this line, i.e. one side of the line will be a mirror image of the other.

64

e.g.

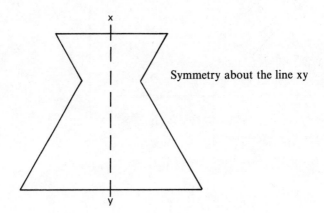

Symmetry about the line xy

(b) Symmetry about a Point
In this case there is a point of symmetry which means that for every line passing through this point there are two points, one on either side, which are equidistant from it.

e.g.

Symmetry about point O

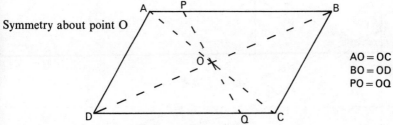

AO = OC
BO = OD
PO = OQ

Simple Scale Drawings
A combination of constructions and bearings are usually necessary to produce these drawings.

Choose simple scales, e.g. $1'' \equiv 5$ km, or 1 cm $\equiv 10$ km etc., and draw a rough diagram first.

e.g. Ship A is 20 km away from a lighthouse L on a bearing of 300° (N60°W) and ship B is 35 km away from the lighthouse on a bearing of 105° (S75°E).

Show this information on a scale drawing and use the drawing to find the distance between ship A and ship B and the bearing of B from A.

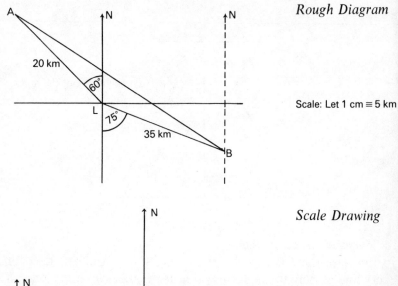

Rough Diagram

Scale: Let 1 cm ≡ 5 km

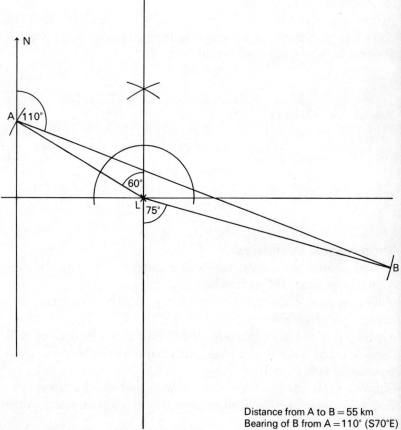

Scale Drawing

Distance from A to B = 55 km
Bearing of B from A = 110° (S70°E)

Part Two

ARITHMETIC

Area and Volume of Pyramid, Cone and Sphere

(a) *Pyramid*

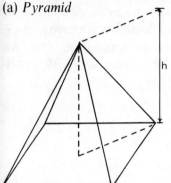

The base can be a triangle, rectangle, square, rhombus, parallelogram, etc.

The surface area can be built up by using what is known of the area of these figures and of the area of a triangle since the side faces are triangular.

$$\text{Volume of pyramid} = \frac{1}{3} \text{ area of base} \times \text{height}$$

(b) *Cone*

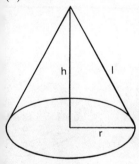

The surface area is made up of the circular base and the curved surface.

$$\text{Area of curved surface} = \pi rl$$

where l is the slant height

$$\text{Total surface area} = \pi r^2 + \pi rl$$

$$\text{Volume of cone} = \frac{1}{3}\pi r^2 h$$

where h is the perpendicular height

(c) *Sphere*

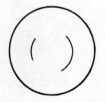

$$\text{Surface area of sphere} = 4\pi r^2$$

$$\text{Volume of sphere} = \frac{4}{3}\pi r^3$$

where r is the radius of the sphere

ALGEBRA

Fractional Equations (with harder denominators)
Method 2   This is the best method to use when the denominators are compound algebraic expressions. The aim is to have a single fraction on each side of the equals sign in an equation, and then get rid of both denominators at the same time by cross-multiplying.

e.g.

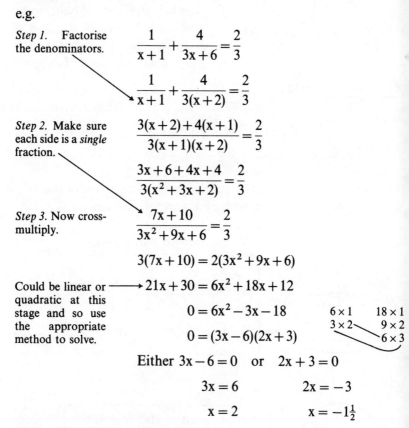

Step 1.   Factorise the denominators.

$$\frac{1}{x+1} + \frac{4}{3x+6} = \frac{2}{3}$$

$$\frac{1}{x+1} + \frac{4}{3(x+2)} = \frac{2}{3}$$

Step 2. Make sure each side is a *single* fraction.

$$\frac{3(x+2)+4(x+1)}{3(x+1)(x+2)} = \frac{2}{3}$$

$$\frac{3x+6+4x+4}{3(x^2+3x+2)} = \frac{2}{3}$$

Step 3. Now cross-multiply.

$$\frac{7x+10}{3x^2+9x+6} = \frac{2}{3}$$

$$3(7x+10) = 2(3x^2+9x+6)$$

Could be linear or quadratic at this stage and so use the appropriate method to solve.

$$21x+30 = 6x^2+18x+12$$

$$0 = 6x^2-3x-18$$

$$0 = (3x-6)(2x+3)$$

6×1	18×1
3×2	9×2
	6×3

Either $3x-6=0$ or $2x+3=0$

$$3x = 6 \qquad\qquad 2x = -3$$

$$x = 2 \qquad\qquad x = -1\tfrac{1}{2}$$

Simultaneous Equations
These equations are solved by substitution.

Step 1. Use the linear equation to obtain one unknown in terms of the other.

68

Step 2. Substitute this value into the quadratic equation.

e.g.

Solve: $y - x = -2$
$\quad\quad x^2 + y^2 + 3x = 7.$

Step 1:
$$y - x = -2$$
$$\therefore \quad y = x - 2$$

Step 2:
$$x^2 + y^2 + 3x = 7$$
$$x^2 + (x-2)^2 + 3x = 7$$
$$x^2 + x^2 - 4x + 4 + 3x = 7$$
$$2x^2 - x - 3 = 0$$
$$(2x - 3)(x + 1) = 0$$

Either $2x - 3 = 0$ or $x + 1 = 0$

$\quad\quad\quad 2x = 3 \quad\quad\quad\quad x = -1$

$\quad\quad\quad x = 1\tfrac{1}{2}$

Substitute for y $\quad$ $y = x - 2$

$\therefore \quad$ If $x = 1\tfrac{1}{2}$, $\quad y = 1\tfrac{1}{2} - 2 = -\tfrac{1}{2}$

and $\quad$ if $x = -1$, $\quad y = -1 - 2 = -3$

$\therefore \quad$ The two pairs of answers are: $\left.\begin{matrix} x = 1\tfrac{1}{2} \\ y = -\tfrac{1}{2} \end{matrix}\right\}$ or $\left.\begin{matrix} x = -1 \\ y = -3 \end{matrix}\right\}$.

Remainder Theorem

This is based on the pattern of a normal division question. If $x^3 - 3x^2 + 2x - 4$ is divided by $(x - 2)$, then an answer can be expected (the quotient Q) plus possibly a remainder.

i.e. $\quad x^3 - 3x^2 + 2x - 4 \equiv Q(x - 2) + R$

Since this is an identity it is satisfied for all values of 'x'.
If $x = 2$, then $(x - 2) = 0$ $\therefore$ $Q(x - 2) = 0$

i.e. $\qquad 8-12+4-4 \equiv Q(0)+R$

$$-4 = R.$$

This theorem is especially useful when the remainder is zero since this means that a factor of the expression has been found; i.e. the first factor can be found by trying different values of 'x' until one is found that makes 'R' zero.

e.g. $\quad$ Factorise $x^3 - 6x^2 + 11x - 6$.

$\qquad$ Put $x = 1 \qquad x^3 - 6x^2 + 11x - 6 = 1 - 6 + 11 - 6 = 0$

$\therefore \qquad (x-1)$ is a factor.

Using long division:

$$\begin{array}{r} x^2 - 5x + 6 \\ x-1 \overline{\smash{\big)}\ x^3 - 6x^2 + 11x - 6} \\ \underline{x^3 - x^2} \\ -5x^2 + 11x \\ \underline{-5x^2 + 5x} \\ +6x - 6 \\ \underline{+6x - 6} \\ \cdots \end{array}$$

$\therefore \qquad x^3 - 6x^2 + 11x - 6 = (x-1)(x^2 - 5x + 6)$

$$= (x-1)(x-2)(x-3).$$

It can also be used to find missing coefficients or constants.
e.g. The expression $x^3 + bx + c$ leaves a remainder 1 when divided by $(x-1)$. When the expression is divided by $(x+1)$, the remainder is 3. Find b and c.

Dividing by $(x-1)$, let $x = 1$. Then $1 + b(1) + c = 1 \longleftarrow R.$

$$b + c = 0 \qquad (1).$$

Dividing by $(x+1)$, let $x = -1$. Then $-1 + b(-1) + c = 3 \longleftarrow R.$

$$-b + c = 4 \qquad (2).$$

Now solve the simultaneous equations (1) and (2) for b and c.

Solution of Quadratic Equations which will not Factorise

A typical quadratic equation is $ax^2 + bx + c = 0$ where a, b and c can have any numerical values. By completing the square it can be shown that the solution of this equation is:

$$x = \frac{-b \pm \sqrt{b^2 - 4ac}}{2a}$$

N.B. The whole of the numerator including '$-b$' is divided by 2a.

The formula will give the two possible values of 'x' and is used when factorisation is not possible.

Direct and Inverse Variation

Direct variation   The statement that y is proportional to x (often written $y \propto x$) means that the graph of y against x is a straight line passing through the origin.

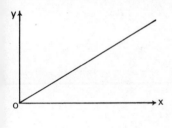

If the gradient of this line is 'k', then $y = kx$.
The value of k is called the *constant of proportionality*.
Therefore the ratio of y to x is equal to k, and y is said to vary directly as x.

A typical question is: If y is directly proportional to x and $y = 2$ when $x = 5$, find the value of y when $x = 6$.

Answer:

$y \propto x$	If $x = 6$, $y = kx$
$\therefore \quad y = kx$	$y = \frac{2}{5} \cdot 6$ (using k from 1st part)
$2 = k(5)$	$y = \frac{12}{5} = 2\frac{2}{5}$
$\frac{2}{5} = k$	

Also if y is proportional to x^2, then $y \propto x^2$ which means $y = kx^2$.

Inverse Variation   If y is inversely proportional to x, then the graph of y against $\frac{1}{x}$ is a straight line passing through the origin.

71

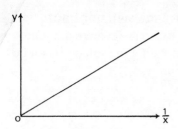

i.e. $y \propto \dfrac{1}{x}$. If the gradient of the line

is 'k', then $y = k \cdot \dfrac{1}{x} = \dfrac{k}{x}$.

e.g. S varies inversely as T^3, and $S = 54$ when $T = 3$. Find the value of T when $S = 16$.

$$S \propto \frac{1}{T^3}$$

$$\therefore \quad S = \frac{k}{T^3}$$

$$54 = \frac{k}{27}$$

$$1458 = k$$

If $S = 16$ $S = \dfrac{k}{T^3}$

$$16 = \frac{1458}{T^3}$$

$$T^3 = \frac{1458}{16} = \frac{729}{8}$$

$$T = \sqrt[3]{\frac{729}{8}} = \frac{9}{2}$$

$$\therefore \ T = 4.5$$

Further Graph Work

It is necessary to be able to plot the graph of a quadratic or cuboid function from a given table of values *or* from a compiled table of values, given the initial values of 'x'.

It is essential to be able to use these graphs to:

(a) find the maximum or minimum values of the function;

(b) solve a quadratic equation;

(c) solve other equations by writing the new equations in the form of the graph plotted.

Also, by plotting two graphs on the same axes, it should be possible to use these graphs to solve a third equation formed by equating the equations of the original graphs. Remember that graphs are equal at their points of intersection.

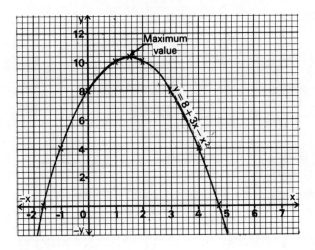

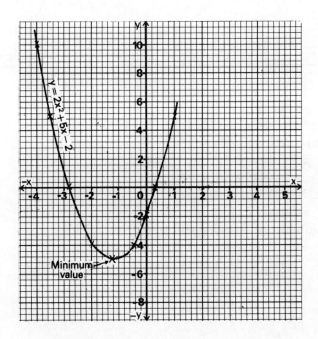

73

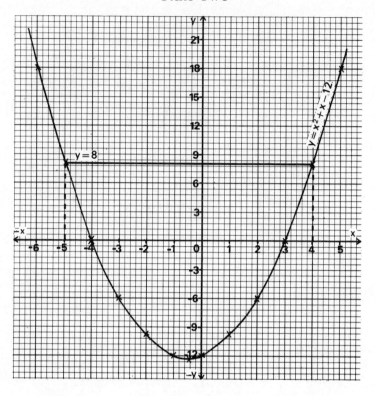

Graph plotted: $x^2 + x - 12 = y$.
To solve $\quad\quad x^2 + x - 12 = 0$,
solutions are found where $y = 0$.
$\therefore \quad\quad x = -4$ or $+3$.
To solve $x^2 + x - 20 = 0$,
rewrite in the form of the graph
$\quad\quad x^2 + x - 12 = 8$,
and solutions are found where $y = 8$.
$\therefore \quad\quad x = -5$ or $+4$.

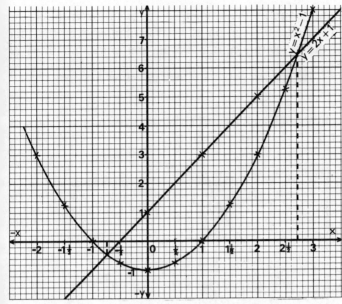

To solve $x^2 - 2x = 2$, equate the graphs plotted.

$x^2 - 1 = 2x + 1$ $\qquad$ $x^2 - 2x = 2$

The solutions are found where the graphs are equal, i.e. where they intersect.

$\therefore$ Solutions are $x = -0.7$ or $+2.7$

Velocity/Time Graph

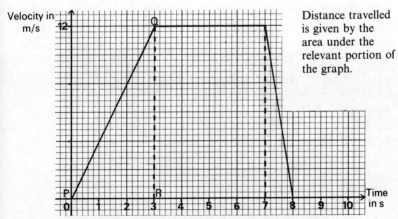

Distance travelled is given by the area under the relevant portion of the graph.

Distance travelled in 3 seconds = Area of $\triangle$PQR
$$= \tfrac{1}{2} \times 3 \times 12 = 18 \text{ metres.}$$

75

Acceleration is given by the gradient or slope of the graph at the relevant time. Since the graph is a straight line over the first 3 seconds, the acceleration is uniform, and since the slope of $PQ = \dfrac{12}{3} = 4$, the acceleration is 4 metres per second per second or 4 m/s².

If the acceleration is not uniform, then it is given by the slope of the tangent to the curve at a given time.

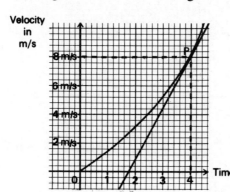

If a tangent is drawn to the curve at the point P, then the gradient of the tangent will be the same as the gradient of the curve at that point.

Acceleration at $P = \dfrac{8}{2\frac{1}{4}} \approx 3.6$ m/s².

Area under a Curve using Strips

The question will usually state how many strips to use and will often state where the dividing lines should be.

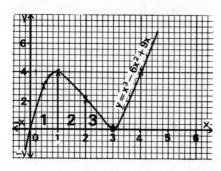

Estimate the area between the curve and the 'x' axis from $x = 0$ to $x = 3$, using 3 strips. (Obvious divisions occur at $x = 1$ and $x = 2$.)

Area of strip $1 = \frac{1}{2} \times 1 \times 4 = 2$ square units.

Area of strip $2 = \frac{1}{2}(4+2).1 = 3$ square units.

Area of strip $3 = \frac{1}{2} \times 1 \times 2 = 1$ square unit.

  Total area $= 6$ square units.

Further Work on Matrices

As with division of a matrix by a scalar, the process of dividing one matrix by another is avoided by multiplying by the reciprocal matrix or *inverse matrix*.

To find the inverse matrix the *determinant* needs to be known and for a 2×2 matrix this can be remembered as a simple formula.

For the matrix $\begin{pmatrix} a & b \\ c & d \end{pmatrix}$ the determinant $D = (ad - bc)$.

Example 1.

$$\text{For } \begin{pmatrix} 4 & 2 \\ 3 & 1 \end{pmatrix} D = (4 \times 1) - (2 \times 3) = 4 - 6 = -2.$$

Example 2.

$$\text{For } \begin{pmatrix} 4 & 3 \\ 1 & 2 \end{pmatrix} D = (4 \times 2) - (3 \times 1) = 8 - 3 = 5.$$

The Inverse Matrix (when $D \neq 0$)

The pattern for the inverse matrix is easy to learn. First consider the general matrix $\begin{pmatrix} a & b \\ c & d \end{pmatrix}$; then to find the inverse the matrix is pre-multiplied by the reciprocal of the determinant (D); 'a' and 'd' are transposed and the signs of 'b' and 'c' are reversed.

i.e.   Inverse $\begin{pmatrix} a & b \\ c & d \end{pmatrix} = \frac{1}{D} \cdot \begin{pmatrix} d & -b \\ -c & a \end{pmatrix}$

e.g.   For $\begin{pmatrix} 4 & 3 \\ 1 & 2 \end{pmatrix}$, $D = 5$. $\therefore \frac{1}{D} = \frac{1}{5}$ $\therefore$ Inverse $= \frac{1}{5} \cdot \begin{pmatrix} 2 & -3 \\ -1 & 4 \end{pmatrix}$

When multiplied out this gives $\begin{pmatrix} \frac{2}{5} & -\frac{3}{5} \\ -\frac{1}{5} & \frac{4}{5} \end{pmatrix}$.

The inverse of a matrix A is written as A^{-1}, and using the above example to check, we find that $A.A^{-1} = A^{-1}.A$; i.e. this product is commutative.

$$\begin{matrix} A & A^{-1} \end{matrix}$$

$$\begin{pmatrix} 4 & 3 \\ 1 & 2 \end{pmatrix}\begin{pmatrix} \frac{2}{5} & -\frac{3}{5} \\ -\frac{1}{5} & \frac{4}{5} \end{pmatrix} = \begin{pmatrix} 1 & 0 \\ 0 & 1 \end{pmatrix} \quad \text{and}$$

$$\begin{matrix} A^{-1} & A \end{matrix}$$

$$\begin{pmatrix} \frac{2}{5} & -\frac{3}{5} \\ -\frac{1}{5} & \frac{4}{5} \end{pmatrix}\begin{pmatrix} 4 & 3 \\ 1 & 2 \end{pmatrix} = \begin{pmatrix} 1 & 0 \\ 0 & 1 \end{pmatrix}$$

i.e. $A.A^{-1} = I = A^{-1}.A$ where I is the unit matrix.

When $D = 0$ the matrix does not have an inverse and is said to be *singular*.

Solution of Simultaneous Equations using Matrices

Any linear equations in two unknowns can be written in matrix form as follows.

$$\begin{matrix} 2p+q=8 \\ 5p-q=6 \end{matrix} \quad \text{can be written as} \quad \begin{pmatrix} 2 & 1 \\ 5 & -1 \end{pmatrix}\begin{pmatrix} p \\ q \end{pmatrix} = \begin{pmatrix} 8 \\ 6 \end{pmatrix}.$$

In order to find $\begin{pmatrix} p \\ q \end{pmatrix}$, the column matrix $\begin{pmatrix} 8 \\ 6 \end{pmatrix}$ has to be pre-multiplied by the inverse of the matrix $\begin{pmatrix} 2 & 1 \\ 5 & -1 \end{pmatrix}$.

$$D = (2 \times -1) - (1 \times 5) = -2 - 5 = -7$$

Be very careful with signs when working out the determinant.

$$\therefore \quad \text{Inverse} = -\frac{1}{7}\begin{pmatrix} -1 & -1 \\ -5 & 2 \end{pmatrix}$$

$$\therefore \quad \begin{pmatrix} p \\ q \end{pmatrix} = -\frac{1}{7}\begin{pmatrix} -1 & -1 \\ -5 & 2 \end{pmatrix}\begin{pmatrix} 8 \\ 6 \end{pmatrix} = -\frac{1}{7}\begin{pmatrix} -14 \\ -28 \end{pmatrix} = \begin{pmatrix} +2 \\ +4 \end{pmatrix}$$

$$\therefore \quad p = 2 \text{ and } q = 4.$$

VECTORS

Quantities which have both magnitude (or size) and direction are known as *vectors*.

For example:
1. The movement (or displacement) from one point to another.
2. Velocity, which is speed in a definite direction.
3. Any force acting in a given direction.

Quantities such as length, time and temperature which have magnitude only are called *scalars*.

Representation of Vectors

Simple straight line diagrams can be used to illustrate vectors, the magnitude and direction of the vector being represented by the length and direction of the line respectively.

(a)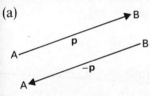

The line AB represents the displacement from A to B which can be written as $\overrightarrow{AB}$ or **p** or **AB**.

The arrow indicates the direction of the movement.

The reverse displacement is written $\overrightarrow{BA}$ or $-\overrightarrow{AB}$ or $-$**p**, i.e. $\overrightarrow{BA}$ is the inverse of $\overrightarrow{AB}$. It is the vector which is equal in magnitude to $\overrightarrow{AB}$ but opposite in direction.

(b) A ship moves a distance of 10 km on a bearing of 062°. This vector quantity can be represented by a scale drawing.

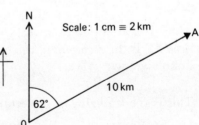

Equal Vectors

If two vectors have the same magnitude and the same direction then they are equal vectors.

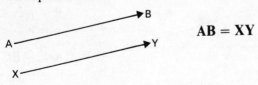

AB = XY

Multiplication by a Scalar

The vector k**b**, where k is a real number, is a vector which has the same direction as **b** but with a magnitude k times that of **b**, i.e. they are parallel.

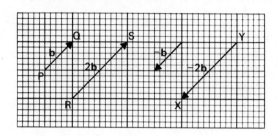

Therefore two vectors are parallel if one is a scalar multiple of the other. **RS** is parallel to **PQ** and has the same direction, whereas **XY** is parallel to **PQ** but is opposite in direction.

Therefore for two vectors to have the same direction, one of them must be a *positive* scalar multiple of the other.

Vector Addition

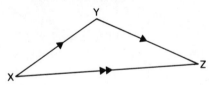

The single displacement which achieves the same effect as two other successive displacements is said to be the sum of the two displacements.

i.e. The arrows on the vectors **XY** and **YZ** follow nose to tail, thus **XZ** is the *resultant* of these two vectors and is marked with a double arrow.

$$XY + YZ = XZ$$

This is the *triangle law* of vector addition.

Subtraction is defined as the addition of a negative vector.

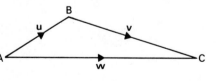

$$AB = AC + CB$$
$$AB = AC + (-BC)$$
$$u = w - v$$

Also $CA = -BC + (-AB)$
$$-w = -v - u$$

Think of the movement as a journey; then the order of the letters tells you the direction you are to take. For example **AB** means you move from A to B whereas **BA** means you move from B to A. If the path you must take is against the direction indicated by the arrow then the sign of the vector is negative.

The *parallelogram law* is equivalent to the triangle law for the addition of vectors and states that:

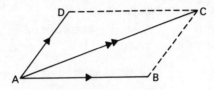

AB + AD = AC

The two laws are equivalent since **AD = BC**.

Any number of vectors may be added.

e.g.

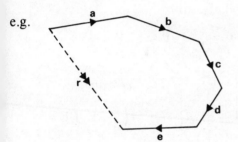

The resultant vector
r = a + b + c + d + e

The addition of vectors is commutative. As shown in the diagrams alongside, the resultant **r** is the same whether **x** is added to **y** or **y** is added to **x**.

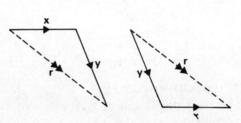

A resultant displacement is zero when the total movement is back to the starting point.

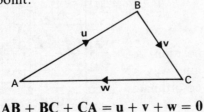

AB + BC + CA = u + v + w = 0

81

Column Vectors

The displacement **AB** is the resultant, or sum, of a horizontal displacement of 3 and a vertical displacement of 4. These displacements are the *components* of the vector and can be expressed as a column vector.

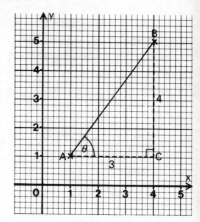

$\mathbf{AB} = \begin{pmatrix} 3 \\ 4 \end{pmatrix}$ with the x component above the y component.

The vector is completely described by the column vector since the magnitude of **AB** can be found using Pythagoras' Theorem, and the direction can be given relative to the x-axis.

$$AB^2 = 3^2 + 4^2 \qquad \text{and} \quad \tan \theta = \frac{4}{3} \quad \therefore \theta \approx 53.1°$$
$$AB = \sqrt{25} = 5$$

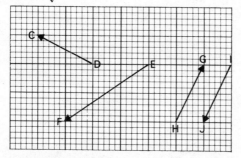

Further examples:

$$\mathbf{DC} = \begin{pmatrix} -2 \\ 1 \end{pmatrix} \qquad \mathbf{EF} = \begin{pmatrix} -3 \\ -2 \end{pmatrix}$$

$$\mathbf{HG} = \begin{pmatrix} 1 \\ 2 \end{pmatrix} \qquad \mathbf{IJ} = \begin{pmatrix} -1 \\ -2 \end{pmatrix}$$

Position Vectors

For any displacement vector which starts at the origin 0 the components are the co-ordinates of the other point.

e.g. The vector $\mathbf{OA} = \begin{pmatrix} 1 \\ 2 \end{pmatrix}$ specifies the position of point A in the same way as the cartesian co-ordinates (1, 2).

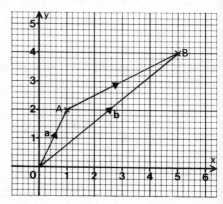

Also if A is (1, 2) and B is (5, 4), the displacement **AB** can be obtained by subtracting the column vector for **OA** from the column vector for **OB**.

$$\mathbf{AB} = \begin{pmatrix} 5 \\ 4 \end{pmatrix} - \begin{pmatrix} 1 \\ 2 \end{pmatrix} = \begin{pmatrix} 4 \\ 2 \end{pmatrix}$$

Adding vectors by constructing a polygon of vectors is time-consuming and often inaccurate; but addition and subtraction using the column vectors is simple since the column vectors obey the same rules as matrices, i.e. the corresponding elements are added or subtracted.

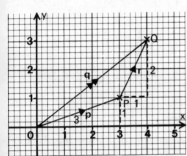

$$\mathbf{q} = \mathbf{p} + \mathbf{r} = \begin{pmatrix} 4 \\ 3 \end{pmatrix}$$

which could have been obtained by adding the corresponding components.

$$\begin{pmatrix} 3 \\ 1 \end{pmatrix} + \begin{pmatrix} 1 \\ 2 \end{pmatrix} = \begin{pmatrix} 4 \\ 3 \end{pmatrix}$$

Also the position vector of the point Q can be obtained by adding the column vector **PQ** to the position vector of the point P.

$$\begin{array}{ccc} \mathbf{OP} & \mathbf{PQ} & \mathbf{OQ} \end{array}$$
i.e.
$$\begin{pmatrix} 3 \\ 1 \end{pmatrix} + \begin{pmatrix} 1 \\ 2 \end{pmatrix} = \begin{pmatrix} 4 \\ 3 \end{pmatrix}$$

∴ The co-ordinates of Q are (4, 3).

Examples of Examination Questions on Vectors

(1) ABCD is a quadrilateral in which A is the point (2, 1), B is (6, 3), D is (1, 4) and $\mathbf{BC} = \begin{pmatrix} -2 \\ 6 \end{pmatrix}$.

Calculate (i) the co-ordinates of C;

(ii) the vector **AD** in the form $\begin{pmatrix} x \\ y \end{pmatrix}$.

State the geometrical relationship between **AD** and **BC**.

83

(i)
$$\overset{\text{OB}}{\begin{pmatrix} 6 \\ 3 \end{pmatrix}} + \overset{\text{BC}}{\begin{pmatrix} -2 \\ 6 \end{pmatrix}} = \overset{\text{OC}}{\begin{pmatrix} 4 \\ 9 \end{pmatrix}}$$

The co-ordinates of C are (4, 9).

(ii)
$$\overset{\text{OD}}{\begin{pmatrix} 1 \\ 4 \end{pmatrix}} - \overset{\text{OA}}{\begin{pmatrix} 2 \\ 1 \end{pmatrix}} = \overset{\text{AD}}{\begin{pmatrix} -1 \\ 3 \end{pmatrix}}$$

The vector **AD** in the form $\begin{pmatrix} x \\ y \end{pmatrix}$ is $\begin{pmatrix} -1 \\ 3 \end{pmatrix}$.

$$\mathbf{AD} = \begin{pmatrix} -1 \\ 3 \end{pmatrix} \text{ and } \mathbf{BC} = \begin{pmatrix} -2 \\ 6 \end{pmatrix} = 2\begin{pmatrix} -1 \\ 3 \end{pmatrix}$$

$\therefore$ **BC** = 2**AD**

Also since **BC** is a scalar multiple of **AD**, then the two vectors must be parallel.

The question can also be answered graphically, as shown.

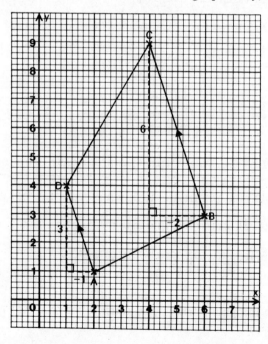

(2)(a) In the triangle PQR, P has co-ordinates $(2, 1)$, Q has co-ordinates $(4, 6)$ and $PR = \begin{pmatrix} 5 \\ 3 \end{pmatrix}$.

Calculate (i) the co-ordinates of R;

(ii) the vector **PQ** in the form $\begin{pmatrix} x \\ y \end{pmatrix}$.

(b) ABCD is a quadrilateral with $AB = 2r - 2s$, $AD = 8r + 6s$ and $AC = 6r + s$.

Calculate **BC** and **CD** in terms of **r** and **s**. Show that $AD = kBC$, and find k.

(a) (i)
$$\overset{\textbf{OP}}{\begin{pmatrix} 2 \\ 1 \end{pmatrix}} + \overset{\textbf{PR}}{\begin{pmatrix} 5 \\ 3 \end{pmatrix}} = \overset{\textbf{OR}}{\begin{pmatrix} 7 \\ 4 \end{pmatrix}} \qquad \therefore \text{ R is the point } (7, 4).$$

(ii)
$$\overset{\textbf{OQ}}{\begin{pmatrix} 4 \\ 6 \end{pmatrix}} - \overset{\textbf{OP}}{\begin{pmatrix} 2 \\ 1 \end{pmatrix}} = \overset{\textbf{PQ}}{\begin{pmatrix} 2 \\ 5 \end{pmatrix}} \qquad \therefore \textbf{PQ} = \begin{pmatrix} 2 \\ 5 \end{pmatrix}$$

(b)

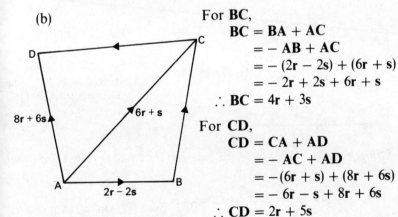

For **BC**,
$$\begin{aligned} \textbf{BC} &= \textbf{BA} + \textbf{AC} \\ &= -\textbf{AB} + \textbf{AC} \\ &= -(2r - 2s) + (6r + s) \\ &= -2r + 2s + 6r + s \\ \therefore \textbf{BC} &= 4r + 3s \end{aligned}$$

For **CD**,
$$\begin{aligned} \textbf{CD} &= \textbf{CA} + \textbf{AD} \\ &= -\textbf{AC} + \textbf{AD} \\ &= -(6r + s) + (8r + 6s) \\ &= -6r - s + 8r + 6s \\ \therefore \textbf{CD} &= 2r + 5s \end{aligned}$$

For k,
$$\textbf{AD} = 8r + 6s = 2(4r + 3s)$$
and $\textbf{BC} = 4r + 3s$,
therefore $\textbf{AD} = 2\textbf{BC}$.
$$\therefore k = 2$$

GEOMETRY

Theorems

In some geometrical questions formal proof of problems and theorems may be necessary. The following theorems and their converses should be known.

The line joining the mid-points of two sides of a triangle is parallel to and equal to half of the third side.

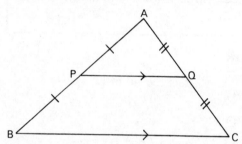

If $AP = PB$ and $AQ = QC$, then $PQ = \frac{1}{2}BC$, and PQ is parallel to BC.

Parallelograms on the same base and between the same parallels are equal in area.

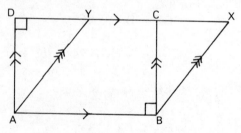

//ogram ABCD = //ogram ABXY in area.

They have the same base AB and lie between the same parallels, AB//DX.

Triangles on the same base and between the same parallels are equal in area.

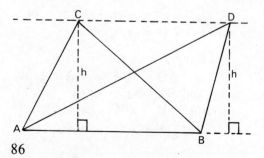

$\triangle ABC = \triangle ABD$ in area.

They have the same base AB and lie between the same parallels, AB//CD.

The angle between a tangent and a chord at the point of contact equals the angle subtended by the chord in the alternate segment.

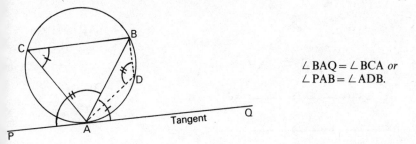

$\angle BAQ = \angle BCA$ *or*
$\angle PAB = \angle ADB$.

If two chords of a circle intersect inside or outside a circle, the product of the segments of one chord is equal to the product of the segments of the other.

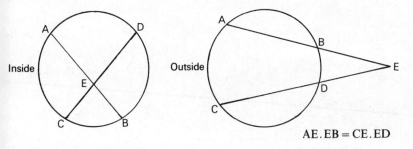

$AE.EB = CE.ED$

If from a point outside a circle two lines are drawn, one a secant and the other a tangent to the circle, then the square on the tangent is equal to the rectangle contained by the whole secant and that part of it outside the circle.

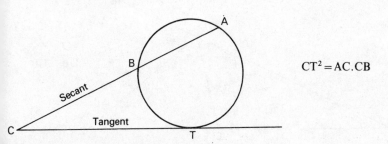

$CT^2 = AC.CB$

A straight line drawn parallel to one side of a triangle divides the other two sides proportionally.

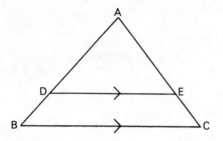

$$\frac{AD}{DB} = \frac{AE}{EC}$$

The internal bisector of an angle of a triangle divides the opposite side internally in the ratio of the sides containing the angle.

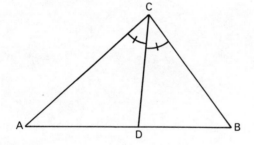

$$\angle ACD = \angle DCB$$
$$\therefore \frac{AD}{DB} = \frac{AC}{CB}$$

Also the external bisector of the angle divides the opposite side in the ratio of the sides containing the angle.

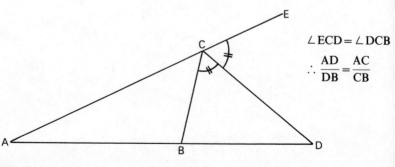

$$\angle ECD = \angle DCB$$
$$\therefore \frac{AD}{DB} = \frac{AC}{CB}$$

Since equal arcs (or chords) subtend equal angles at the centre of the circle the length of an arc must be proportional to the angle it subtends at the centre.

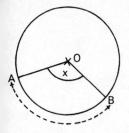

The length of arc $AB = \dfrac{x}{360}$ of the circumference of the whole circle.

Latitude and Longitude

The following diagram gives the main terms which should be known.

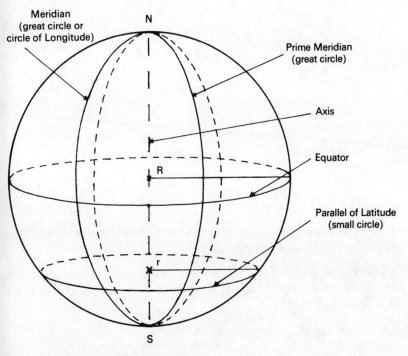

'R' is the radius of the earth.
'r' is the radius of a plane of latitude.

If λ is the angle of latitude then $\boxed{r = R \cos \lambda}$.

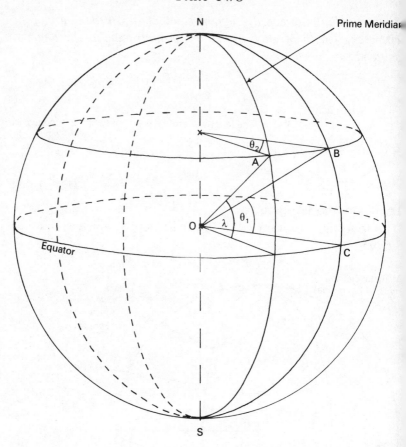

Arcs of great circles are fractions of the circumference of the earth itself, i.e. fractions of $2\pi R$.

However, arcs of circles of latitude other than the equator are fractions of circles with circumference $2\pi r$ or $2\pi R \cos \lambda$, since $r = R \cos \lambda$.

i.e.   In the diagram shown:

$$\text{Arc } BC = \frac{\theta_1}{360} . 2\pi R \qquad \text{since BC lies on a great circle;}$$

and $$\text{Arc } AB = \frac{\theta_2}{360} . 2\pi R \cos \lambda. \qquad \text{since AB lies on a circle of latitude.}$$

TRIGONOMETRY

Trigonometric Ratios
The following distinction should be borne in mind.

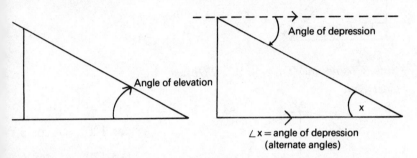

The trigonometric ratios for a right-angled triangle are as follows:

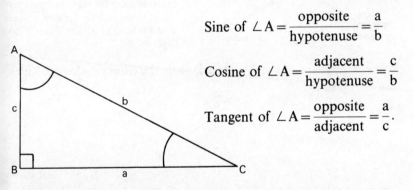

$$\text{Sine of } \angle A = \frac{\text{opposite}}{\text{hypotenuse}} = \frac{a}{b}$$

$$\text{Cosine of } \angle A = \frac{\text{adjacent}}{\text{hypotenuse}} = \frac{c}{b}$$

$$\text{Tangent of } \angle A = \frac{\text{opposite}}{\text{adjacent}} = \frac{a}{c}.$$

Abbreviations as follows:

$$\sin \angle C = \frac{\text{opp.}}{\text{hyp.}} = \frac{c}{b} \; ; \quad \cos \angle C = \frac{\text{adj.}}{\text{hyp.}} = \frac{a}{b} \; ;$$

$$\tan \angle C = \frac{\text{opp.}}{\text{adj.}} = \frac{c}{a}.$$

It is necessary to be able to use trigonometric ratios in the solution of right-angled triangles. A calculator should be used when necessary.

e.g.

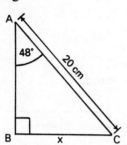

$$\frac{x}{20} = \sin 48°$$

$$x = 20 \times 0.743144825$$

$$x = 14.86289651 \text{ cm}$$

$$x \approx 14.9 \text{ cm}$$

∠C can be found using angle sum of triangle.

AB can now be found using Pythagoras' Theorem.

Sine, Cosine and Tangent of an Obtuse Angle:
Cast Rule

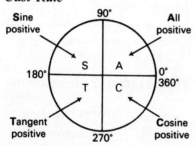

e.g.

$$\sin 120° = \sin 60°$$

$$\cos 120° = -\cos 60°$$

$$\tan 120° = -\tan 60°$$

The *cast rule* is a simple way of remembering the sign changes that occur when finding the sine, cosine and tangent of angles from 0° to 360°.

If the triangle is not right-angled, then the Sine or Cosine Rules can be used.

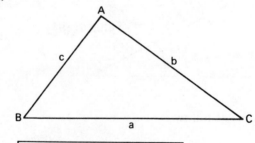

Sine Rule

$$\frac{a}{\sin A} = \frac{b}{\sin B} = \frac{c}{\sin C}$$

Cosine Rule

$$\cos A = \frac{b^2 + c^2 - a^2}{2bc}$$

$$\text{or } a^2 = b^2 + c^2 - 2bc.\cos A$$

These formulae are easily rearranged for cos B, b^2, cos C, c^2.
The trigonometric formula for the area of a triangle is as follows:

$$\text{Area of triangle} = \tfrac{1}{2}a.b.\sin C$$

$$\text{or} = \tfrac{1}{2}b.c.\sin A$$

$$\text{or} = \tfrac{1}{2}a.c.\sin B.$$

Surd Values

Surd Values for sin, cos and tan of 45°, 60°, 30°.

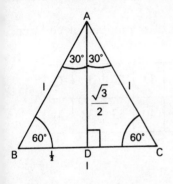

By Pythagoras $AD = \dfrac{\sqrt{3}}{2}$

$$\sin 60° = \dfrac{\sqrt{3}}{2} \qquad \sin 30° = \dfrac{1}{2}$$

$$\cos 60° = \dfrac{1}{2} \qquad \cos 30° = \dfrac{\sqrt{3}}{2}$$

$$\tan 60° = \sqrt{3} \qquad \tan 30° = \dfrac{1}{\sqrt{3}}$$

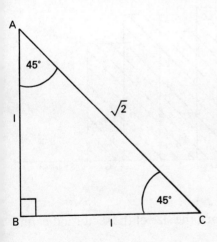

$$\sin 45° = \dfrac{1}{\sqrt{2}}$$

$$\cos 45° = \dfrac{1}{\sqrt{2}}$$

$$\tan 45° = 1$$

93

STATISTICS

The collection and analysis of data is known as statistics. Tables and diagrams are used constantly to present facts. Some of the main methods of presentation are as follows.

Simple Bar Chart

Information is represented by bars or blocks usually drawn vertically.

e.g. The table shows the mass in kg of a number of children, each identified by a letter.

Child's Initial	A	B	C	D	E	F	G
Mass in kg	25	30	37	40	33	38	31

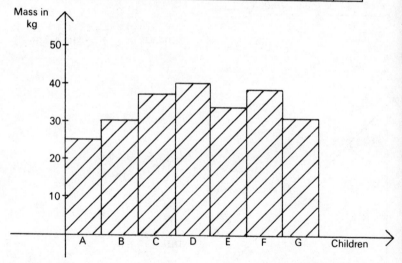

Pie Chart

This is a circle divided into sectors, the size of the sector indicating the proportion of the total.

e.g.   The household expenditure for a week is £80. £32 is spent on food, £16 on heating and lighting, £8 on rent, £12 on rates and £12 on miscellaneous items. Draw a pie chart to represent these facts.

The full circle contains 360° and so, first of all, the sector angles must be calculated. There are several ways of doing this but perhaps the simplest way in this case is to find out what angle will represent £1.

£80 is represented by 360°.

£1 is represented by $\dfrac{360°}{80} = \dfrac{9°}{2}$.

Therefore the sector angles are as follows:

For £32 the angle is $32 \times \dfrac{9°}{2} = 144°$.

For £16 the angle is $16 \times \dfrac{9°}{2} = 72°$.

For £8 the angle is $8 \times \dfrac{9°}{2} = 36°$.

For £12 the angle is $12 \times \dfrac{9°}{2} = 54°$.

The circle can now be divided up using a protractor. Pie charts are useful provided there are not too many parts. They lose their effectiveness if the sectors become too small.

Histogram

This is a diagram which is used to represent a frequency distribution. Care should be taken not to confuse it with a bar chart. In this case it is the area of the rectangles or bars which represents the frequencies of the various classes. If all the classes or groups have the same width, then so will the rectangles or bars, and the frequencies will be represented by their heights.

e.g.

Mass of pies to the nearest gram	Number of pies of this mass (frequency)
200 g	5
199 g	12
198 g	16
197 g	20
196 g	9
195 g	4
	Total 66

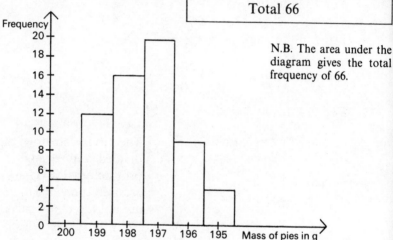

N.B. The area under the diagram gives the total frequency of 66.

The Mean of a Frequency Distribution

When finding the arithmetic mean, divide the total of the quantities by the number of quantities. However, when finding the mean of a frequency distribution, the frequencies as well as the measurements must be taken into account.

Consider the example about the pies; then the mean mass will be found as follows.

Mean mass

$$= \frac{(200 \times 5) + (199 \times 12) + (198 \times 16) + (197 \times 20) + (196 \times 9) + (195 \times 4)}{66}$$

$$= \frac{1000 + 2388 + 3168 + 3940 + 1764 + 780}{66}$$

$$= \frac{13\,040}{66} \approx 197.6 \text{ g}.$$

The Median
The median is the value which lies half-way along the series when the values are arranged in ascending or descending order of size.

Taking the following list of numbers 2, 3, 3, 5, 6, 7, 7, then the median is 5 because there are three numbers below this value and three numbers above it.

However, if the list has an even number of values the median is found by taking the mean of the two middle values.

e.g.   In the list 3, 4, 6, 8, 9, 9, the median is

$$\frac{6+8}{2} = \frac{14}{2} = 7.$$

The Mode
The mode is the value which occurs most often, i.e. the most common value. The mode for the pie masses is therefore 197 g since it occurs most frequently.

It is possible to have more than one mode where there are two or more values that occur the same number of times.

Similarly, if all the values occur the same number of times, then no mode exists.

Frequency Polygons
Frequency polygons may be used to compare two distributions and this is their main advantage over histograms.

Data for histograms is often presented in classes or groups and the points plotted for a frequency polygon are the mid-points of these class intervals. In order to complete the polygon an extra interval is added at each end.

e.g.   Consider the heights of 50 men as shown in the table below:

Height of men in cm	170–174	175–179	180–184	185–189	190–194	195–199
Frequency	4	8	11	15	9	3

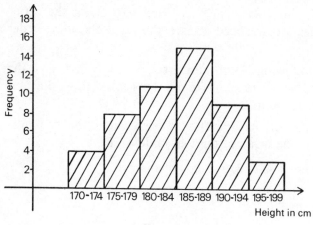

Histogram

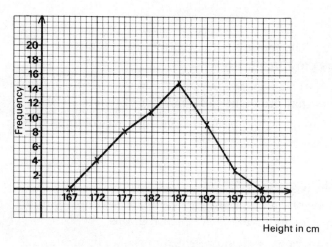

Height in cm

Frequency Polygon

Cumulative Frequency

In many investigations the information required is "how many are more than ..." or "how many earn less than ...". A cumulative frequency table readily gives the answers to such questions because it presents a running total. Using the information from the previous example the cumulative frequency table will be as follows.

Height cm	Frequency f	Height less than	Cumulative Frequency
170–174	4	174.5	4
175–179	8	179.5	12
180–184	11	184.5	23
185–189	15	189.5	38
190–194	9	194.5	47
195–199	3	199.5	50

A cumulative frequency table can be illustrated by plotting a graph known as a *cumulative frequency curve or ogive*.

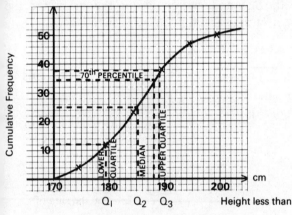

Cumulative Frequency Ogive

One quarter of the men have heights less than or equal to 179.8 cm. This height is known as the *lower quartile* (Q_1).

The *median* (Q_2) can easily be found from the ogive. Half the men have heights under 185.5 cm.

One quarter of the men have heights greater than or equal to 189.4 cm. This height is known as the *upper quartile* (Q_3).

The height 188.5 cm is known as the *70th percentile* or *7th decile* since 70% (35) have heights under 188.5 cm.

The 25th, 50th and 75th percentiles correspond to Q_1, Q_2 and Q_3 respectively.

Dispersion
This is the way in which the data are spread or dispersed between the upper and lower limits. The difference between these limits is called the *range*.

A common measure of the dispersion is the *semi-interquartile range* which is obtained from Q_1 and Q_3 of the cumulative frequency ogive.

i.e.   Semi-interquartile range $= \dfrac{Q_3 - Q_1}{2}$.

Mean Deviation

This is another method of measuring dispersion about some central point, e.g. the mean or the median. It does not take account of whether the deviation is positive or negative.

e.g.   Calculate the mean deviation about the mean for the following set of marks: 34, 41, 53, 53, 56, 60, 64, 71.

The mean for the set is 54.

Set of Marks	Deviation from mean ignoring signs $\lvert d \rvert$
34	20
41	13
53	1
53	1
56	2
60	6
64	10
71	17
	$\Sigma \lvert d \rvert = 70$

[N = the number of items in the set.]

$\therefore$ Mean deviation about the mean for the set of marks

$= \dfrac{\Sigma \lvert d \rvert}{N}$ (Σ being 'the sum of')

$= \dfrac{70}{8}$

$= 8.75.$

A small mean deviation about the mean indicates a greater consistency than a large mean deviation about the mean.

The Assumed Mean

The numbers involved in a frequency distribution can often be large or awkward and a lot of time and effort can be saved by using an assumed mean.

e.g.   5 pies have mass 200 g, 12 have mass 199 g, 16 have mass 198 g, 20 have mass 197 g, 9 have mass 196 g, 4 have mass 195 g. Find the mean mass of the pies.

Let the assumed mean A = 197 g.

100

Mass of pies x	Deviation $d = x - A$	Frequency f	fd
200	3	5	15 ⎫
199	2	12	24 ⎪
198	1	16	16 ⎬ + 55
197	0	20	0 ⎭
196	−1	9	−9 ⎫ −17
195	−2	4	−8 ⎭
		$\Sigma f = 66$	$\Sigma fd = 38$

Mean $\bar{x} = A + \dfrac{\Sigma fd}{\Sigma f} = 197 + \dfrac{38}{66}$

$$= 197 + 0.5757$$
$$\approx 197.6 \text{ g}.$$

Variance and Standard Deviation

These are more accurate measures of spread and are used more often. The mean of the squared deviations from the mean is the *variance*. The square root of the variance is known as the *standard deviation*.

e.g. Find the standard deviation of the following numbers: 35, 40, 50, 55, 60.

Variable x	Deviation from mean $x - \bar{x}$	Square of deviations $(x - \bar{x})^2$
35	−13	169
40	−8	64
50	2	4
55	7	49
60	12	144
$\Sigma x = 240$		$\Sigma(x - \bar{x})^2 = 430$

$\bar{x} = \dfrac{\Sigma x}{N} = \dfrac{240}{5}$

$$= 48$$

101

$$\text{Variance} = \frac{\Sigma(x - \bar{x})^2}{N} = \frac{430}{5} = 86$$

$$\therefore \text{Standard Deviation } \sigma = \sqrt{\frac{\Sigma(x - \bar{x})^2}{N}}$$

$$= \sqrt{86} = 9.2736$$

$$= 9.3 \text{ to 1 place of decimals.}$$

If the observations are large or awkward the working can be simplified by using the following formula.

$$\sigma = \sqrt{\frac{\Sigma x^2}{N} - \left(\frac{\Sigma x}{N}\right)^2}$$

To find the standard deviation of a frequency distribution the formula becomes:

$$\sigma = \sqrt{\frac{\Sigma f(x - \bar{x})^2}{\Sigma f}}$$

or $$\sigma = \sqrt{\frac{\Sigma f x^2}{\Sigma f} - \left(\frac{\Sigma f x}{\Sigma f}\right)^2}$$

These calculations can also be further simplified by using an assumed mean. The formula then becomes:

$$\sigma = \sqrt{\frac{\Sigma(x - A)^2}{N} - \left(\frac{\Sigma(x - A)}{N}\right)^2}$$

or $$\sigma = \sqrt{\frac{\Sigma f(x - A)^2}{\Sigma f} - \left(\frac{\Sigma f(x - A)}{\Sigma f}\right)^2} \quad \text{for a frequency distribution.}$$

Probability

Questions are often asked about the probability or chance of a particular event occurring: "What is the probability of drawing a six of hearts from a well-shuffled pack of cards?" or "What is the chance of getting a four with one throw of a die?"

If an event can happen in 'p' ways out of 'q' equally possible ways, then $\dfrac{p}{q}$ is said to be the probability of the event happening.

Likewise, the probability of an event *not* happening is $\dfrac{r}{q}$ if the event fails to happen in 'r' ways out of 'q' equally possible ways.

Clearly $p + r = q$.

A probability of 1 indicates a certain event.

A probability of 0 indicates an impossible event.

The probability of any event is a number between 0 and 1.

e.g.　The probability 'P' of a head on tossing a coin $= \dfrac{1}{2}$.

　　　P of drawing an ace from a pack of cards $= \dfrac{4}{52} = \dfrac{1}{13}$.

　　　P of drawing a spade from a pack of cards $= \dfrac{13}{52} = \dfrac{1}{4}$.

Mutually Exclusive Events

X and Y are mutually exclusive events or disjoint events if the two events cannot take place at the same time.

　　　Then $P(X \text{ or } Y) = P(X) + P(Y)$.

e.g.　$P(\text{ace or queen}) = P(\text{ace}) + P(\text{queen}) = \dfrac{1}{13} + \dfrac{1}{13} = \dfrac{2}{13}$.

Independent Events

If one event has no effect on the other they are said to be independent.

e.g.　If a coin is tossed and a die is thrown, what is the probability of a head and a four?

　　　$P(\text{head and four}) = \dfrac{1}{2} \times \dfrac{1}{6} = \dfrac{1}{12}$.

Tree Diagrams

If a die is thrown twice, what is the probability of getting a four each time, a four first time but not second time, a four the second time but not the first, no four at all?

$$P(\text{four, four}) = \frac{1}{6} \times \frac{1}{6} = \frac{1}{36}$$

$$P(\text{four, not a four}) = \frac{1}{6} \times \frac{5}{6} = \frac{5}{36}$$

$$P(\text{not a four, four}) = \frac{5}{6} \times \frac{1}{6} = \frac{5}{36}$$

$$P(\text{not a four, not a four}) = \frac{5}{6} \times \frac{5}{6} = \frac{25}{36}.$$

N.B. Since all the possibilities are covered then the sum of the probabilities is 1.

Problems of this type can be illustrated by a *tree diagram* as follows:

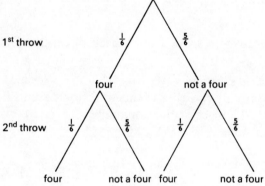

Outcome	2 fours	1 four	1 four	no fours
Probability	$\frac{1}{36}$	$\frac{5}{36}$	$\frac{5}{36}$	$\frac{25}{36}$

The probability of each event is found by multiplying the probabilities along the branches.

i.e. $$P(2 \text{ fours}) = \frac{1}{6} \times \frac{1}{6} = \frac{1}{36}.$$

Also the probability of obtaining only 1 four with two throws of the die is $\frac{5}{36} + \frac{5}{36} = \frac{10}{36} = \frac{5}{18}$.